Rosemary Lain-Priestley is an Anglican priest and a regular contributor to 'Thought for the Day' and 'Act of Worship' on BBC Radio 4. Her current work focuses on developing the ministry of female clergy both locally and nationally. She was previously Associate Vicar of St Martin-in-the-Fields and, prior to that, curate of St Paul's, Scotforth, Lancaster. Before ordination she worked and travelled in South Africa and, before that, was an immigration adviser. She is married with two young daughters and lives in London.

THE COURAGE TO CONNECT

CONNECT

Becoming all we can be

Rosemary Lain-Priestley

First published in Great Britain in 2007

Society for Promoting Christian Knowledge
36 Causton Street
London SW1P 4ST

British Library Cataloguing-in-Publication Data
A catalogue record for this book is available from the British Library

ISBN 978–0–281–05950–8

1 3 5 7 9 10 8 6 4 2

Typeset by Graphicraft Ltd, Hong Kong
Printed in Great Britain by Ashford Colour Press

Produced on paper from sustainable forests

For Antony, who lives life deliberately and with courage.

For Hannah and Olivia, our two graces.

For Dad, who awoke in me the idea of God.

Contents

———◆———

Contents

Acknowledgements

My love and gratitude go to the following people, present and eternally present.

My parents, for telling me a story about God and the world in which I could find myself. My brother, Andrew, for always being there, and for returning me to earth with dry humour.

The congregation of Christ Church, Colne, who encouraged me towards ordination; the people of Scotforth and Over Wyresdale, for teaching me what a deacon and a priest might be.

The clergy and congregation of St Martin-in-the-Fields, for showing me how to wrestle with God in life's realities, and particularly 'the mess in the middle'.

Nicholas Holtam, for being instrumental in two of the best opportunities I've ever had. David Monteith, for the collegiality, adventure and playfulness of those first few years in the big city. Liz Griffiths, for theological partnership and fits of laughter, and Liz Russell, for wisdom and forbearance.

Christine Morgan and the 'Thought for the Day' team for challenging me to know what I think and to say it as well as I can.

Those involved in the Windsor Leadership Trust experience, which at the right moment gave me the confidence to try to do what I dreamed might be possible.

All those who said that a book must be written (and finished), especially Sue Saville, Clare Herbert, Jane Ryan, Briony Martin, Ivy Crawford and (with special thanks for the notebook) Nadine Swaffield.

Alison Barr at SPCK, for helping me to find the particular book that was in me right now, believing I could actually write it, and commissioning me so that I had to.

Those who read the draft, suggested who the readership might be and shared ideas on how the book might find its way to them: Katie Dias, Sarah Shaw, Alison Lyon; and Andrew Caspari, whose invaluable professional advice was enthusiastically and generously given.

Acknowledgements

Douglas Board, for honouring the commitment to read each chapter as it emerged, for perception in highlighting what might be done differently, and for pointing out – when I couldn't see it – the conclusion to which the book was leading.

Friends and relatives too numerous to name, who – whether or not they consider themselves 'religious' – have inspired me through the depth, diversity and connections of their own lives.

And finally the people who are my home. Hannah, whose ideas and questions have taught me so much about God; Olivia, whose strength and directness startle me into wakefulness; and Antony, who eats life, has always believed I can do anything, and still wants to be with me. The three of you give me the love, the space and the courage to connect. Thank you.

Introduction

I went to the woods because I wished to live deliberately, to front only the essential facts of life . . . and not, when I came to die, discover that I had not lived.[1]

Henry David Thoreau

To live deliberately rather than by accident requires great courage and honesty. It means facing raw human experience as it is, without glossing over the difficult bits. But it is the only way to engage with the person we really are – and in doing so to discover something of the mystery of God.

In our search for God we are our own starting point. Our path then spirals outwards, taking in people, places, occasions and events. These ever-widening circles hold the potential for our growth. *The Courage to Connect* therefore reflects on my own experience and the stories of other individuals and communities. From a different standpoint each chapter explores the question: How might we grow consciously into a deeper awareness of God and a fuller understanding of ourselves?

The book tries to unfold some of the issues we face in our search for God, and in our desire to be more comfortable in our own skin. It makes the following suggestions.

Risk, doubt and mortality are fundamental to the fabric of our lives. We need to face head-on what they might mean for us. Envy and the struggle to understand the different aspects of ourselves are painfully necessary for our growth.

Frameworks and authorities might be a good thing – but we need to be grown-up and astute in the way that we respond to them. Our habit of seeking perfection may be damaging if we don't handle it carefully. We should ask ourselves whether we can afford to live at such an exhausting pace – and if the answer is no, do something about it.

If we are to embrace what is strange – in ourselves as well as in others – we will need the courage to celebrate and struggle with difference. Self-understanding is not just a luxury for those who can access good therapy – it is a necessity if we want to live fully.

We should expect to find meaning in the smallest details of our daily experience as well as in the big events of our lives. We need to understand fertility in its broadest and deepest sense, and to learn to challenge what denies life.

None of us achieves our full potential in this lifetime and we are easily deflected from honesty with God, others and ourselves by the insistent and immediate demands of events, relationships and all that we call daily life – in fact by the very things from which we can learn the most.

We are also deflected by fear. The fear that in the end it may all mean nothing. A central conviction of the book is that only by acknowledging and working with that fear – and all of our other 'tough calls' – can we live deliberately, know God and become more fully ourselves.

And only then can God be wholly God. We reflect God in the world, and none of us can do that quite as anyone else can. If we're avoiding what we are, or pretending to be someone else, God's presence is inevitably diminished. In the words of the second-century saint, Irenaeus, 'The glory of God is a [person] fully alive.'[2]

The Courage to Connect suggests that we reflect God most clearly when we pay attention to the world, others and ourselves with honesty and courage. When we are fully alive and fully present. And when we connect. For doing all of this – challenging as it is – is what it means to live life deliberately.

1

In the absence of a Green Room
Risk as a way of life

If we really want to connect with God, pregnancy and labour have much to say about the sort of Creator we might be dealing with. The intimacy of childbirth speaks of a God who knows the reality of human experience in all its grit and glory. The risks suggest familiarity with the fears and precarious hopes that shape us all.

In late 2002, one of my colleagues at St Martin-in-the-Fields church in London wrote a carol service around the theme 'Waiting to be born'. As the only member of the clergy team who had ever given birth, I was allocated the preaching slot. Colleagues helpfully suggested that it might be a good opportunity for me to work through my experience of childbirth from a theological perspective!

Did they know what floodgates they were opening? Most new mothers will tell their birth stories to anyone who will listen – on that occasion I had a captive audience of a thousand . . .

In fact Hannah Sophia Lain was born by emergency Caesarean section and the period of so-called 'natural labour' was very limited. We had little or no choice in the matter, as Hannah would have been unlikely to survive any other way.

Within minutes of the first contractions my husband – with his watchful eye on the several monitors to which I was attached – realized that there was something very wrong. He ran to find a midwife, and what followed was both disorientating and very frightening.

It was also extremely painful. Antenatal midwives allude airily to internal examinations as though the process is on a par with showing the dentist your teeth. They don't tell you how such an examination might feel when carried out by three people in immediate succession in an emergency, with a distressed baby and no pain relief. By the time we got into theatre my only coherent thought was, 'Just get us through this alive'.

So I felt compelled to preach at that carol service about risk as a fundamental and inextricable element of life lived to the full. Or even life lived at all. And what the risk of being born might say about God.

Birth is the primal risk, the one that triggers all other unknown possibilities.

> Her beginning was the still moment
> In a moving tide, dark beyond all
> Discovery . . .[1]

A friend sent us these words a few days after Hannah was born. They are from the poem 'Applied Astronomy', by the late New Zealand poet Lauris Edmond. The poem explores the miracle of human life itself: why it began, where it began, where it might be going. It asks how that life connects with the life that could be above and beyond, before and after, our immediate experience.

At birth we have the first conscious experience of the complexity of the world beyond ourselves. Questions begin to be triggered about who and what we are, who the other beings around us might be and how we might relate to them.

As we begin to explore the world other questions gradually present themselves, such as where we might have come from, where we might be going, and what we might be for. And at some point a little further down the line some of us wonder whether or not there truly is a Creator whom we can name and encounter and love – and by whom we can be named and encountered and loved.

If birth is the biggest risk it is also the biggest miracle. The conception of an individual person means the difference between nothing and everything, between non-being and being, between the void and unlimited potential. Lauris Edmond addresses the newborn child:

> You are the surety
> We need that shocks of birth and death are
> Big bangs only and in between, creation's

Widening circles may carry us perhaps
Beyond the farthest stars.[2]

Perhaps. Let's hope so. We cannot be sure – it's all a bit of a risk.

As our life continues to unfold, so do the risks. They come in all sorts of shapes, forms and levels of importance. Whether we are deciding how to spend our money, with whom to spend our life, whether to change our job, which school to try to get our child into, where to go on holiday or how to handle a particularly difficult issue at work or home, we are taking risks. We know this personally and in our corporate and community lives too.

The management of most organizations is now at least partly shaped by the awareness of risk: how to assess it, how to minimize it, how to live with it, how to make it work for your team, company or institution. Yet if we are to live creatively we must take risks all the time. Because there is much in life that we cannot predict, much that might happen that we cannot imagine and much that we cannot control.

In 2006, the Health and Safety Commission launched a new campaign that ran counter to most people's expectations. The initiative was aimed at organizations that were overemphasizing trivial risks. The chair of the Commission urged those with a tendency to overcaution to 'Get a life'.

The impetus for the campaign seemed to be the Commission's concern that some organizations had developed an approach that was risk averse in the extreme. There had been a rash of reports about schools suspending any off-site extra-curricular activities for fear of accidents, legal action or adverse publicity. Illustrating how far this tendency had developed, one journalist cited a college that warned participants in a field trip to 'Ensure you can see where you're putting your feet before walking'.

For most of us quite a lot of the time, uncertainty lurks just below the surface. We think we can see where we're putting our foot, but in an instant life can shock us, surprise us, even profoundly disorientate us. And on some level we know this. We might not admit to being a neurotic parent, but losing sight of our child in a playground can cause our pulse to race for several minutes *after* they reappear from underneath the climbing frame. We might be reasonably financially secure, but in a culture where jobs

3

are no longer for life – or even for one phase of life – long-term financial commitments have us sweating in the early hours.

As a contributor to Radio 4's 'Thought for the Day', I regularly sit in the Green Room of the *Today* programme at BBC Television Centre. There I meet and observe people who are preparing to be interviewed by the infamously rigorous *Today* programme presenters, who will leave no stone, half-thought or nuance unturned.

Politicians and activists, civil servants and authors – all manner of society's movers and shakers – sit in that Green Room. They read notes and newspapers, listen in to the present debate in the studio and do everything they can to be as ready as possible for what might come.

Later, emerging from the fray, they might grab a strong cup of coffee from the drinks machine, debrief with their aides or exchange a few polite words with the person who was positioned against them in the interview. What each contributor wonders in common is: 'What impact did I make?' 'Will anything that I said be remembered or make a difference?' And probably, 'Could I have been better prepared?'

Watching all this from the sidelines, it strikes me forcibly that life has no Green Room. We arrive at the centre of our own stage unrehearsed, overawed, ignorant of the questions we will be asked and unsure of the motivation of those around us. Do we get the opportunity to debrief with anyone afterwards, to assess our impact, to know whether we made a difference? Maybe. But so far as advance preparation is concerned, there is nothing.

This applies to life as a whole and also in some sense to each new day. Our Blackberries, Palm Pilots and Filofaxes may confidently offer a view on what they expect the hours to hold, but our lives are influenced by much that is beyond our control – there's a lot of room for manoeuvre and we're unaware of where much of it lies. What is for certain is that there's no opportunity to listen in as the day warms up, or to get the measure of where it's going before we live it. We're pretty much in the dark about a lot of things.

And we fear that dark. Our human instinct is to minimize uncertainty and risk. We want to know what is going to happen to us, what our choices might be, where our lives are leading, how things might pan out in any given situation. We want to see clearly, be aware of the facts, be fully prepared and in control of whatever life brings. We don't enjoy the image of ourselves groping for the light switch.

The Jewish and Christian traditions have much to teach us about knowing and not knowing, and often use the image of light and dark to do that. The Scriptures speak of the light of the knowledge of God and the darkness of estrangement. Perhaps most famously on this theme, Isaiah declares 'The people who walked in darkness have seen a great light – those who lived in a land of deep darkness – on them light has shined'.[3]

For human beings – at least those of us who rely on our sense of sight – the lack of sun, moon or artificial light is commonly associated with danger and the unknown. Light makes us feel safe. Our fears are somehow mitigated by the hope that light will return after darkness. So we tell ourselves in dark nights of uncertainty that it will, quite literally, all look better in the morning.

Like all images, this one has its limitations. Its negative aspect is the association of darkness with all that is threatening, perhaps even sinister, when actually darkness can be a very good thing – helpful, even necessary, and rich. The soil is dark and it nurtures untold and fertile possibilities. For the foetus, the darkness of the womb nourishes the potential of all that is to come. And for much of the world's population darkness describes, permeates and expresses what is good about their culture and ethnicity.

This is where the image of darkness becomes helpful in our handling of risk and uncertainty. It reminds us that they too can be fertile ground for our human development, our exploration of our self, our meditation on what it means to be part of the wider creation. We often learn more about ourselves in moments when we are less assured than at times when we think we know exactly where we are going. In these tentative times the darkness compels us to stay in touch with the creative tension of uncertainty and risk. If it keeps us for long enough in one place with only a few thoughts, things that are new and life-giving may be born out of the struggle.

And so again through the prophet Isaiah God promises 'I will give you the treasures of darkness'.[4] Many others since then have recognized the potential of that place. It is beautifully expressed by J. R. R. Tolkien in *The Return of the King*. Frodo, seeing the

5

beauty of Arwen, Evenstar of her people, exclaims: 'At last I understand why we have waited! This is the ending. Now not only day shall be loved, but night too shall be beautiful and blessed . . .'[5]

Uncertainty and risk, while being a salutary reminder that we lack the light of clarity and full knowledge, are inextricably linked with glorious mystery and as yet unexamined potential. They can enable us to look in on ourselves and discover much of God that we had not known was there. They might force us back on resources we did not know we possessed, and they may lead to discoveries we would otherwise not have made.

Human beings can therefore live creatively, even gloriously, with a good deal of uncertainty. And we do so, on a day-to-day basis, in many ways. The risk that perhaps permeates most people's lives most completely is that of relationships. Relationships of any kind – between colleagues, neighbours, friends, lovers, family – are singularly precarious undertakings. To open ourselves to another person, to invite or accept the intertwining of their life with ours, is to make ourselves very vulnerable.

There's generally no Green Room for relationships either. Holding back essentially means not relating. Once we're committed in some way – for instance to the exploration of a friendship or a lifelong partnership – there's everything to lose. And everything to discover.

Each new connection between human beings draws out different character traits, because the chemistry between any two people – or more if we're talking about families, friendship groups or colleagues – will always be unique, untried and untested. We are changed by our interaction with others. And the word chemistry is particularly apt, as relationships are by their very nature experimental, possibly in quite a precarious and even potentially explosive way! We may know what we think or hope the outcome might be, but the chemical reactions can find us unprepared.

It's often when we risk most that we gain and give most. But the decisions that involve the most risk often involve us in a lot of soul-searching and the balancing of a number of significant priorities.

In a remarkable radio programme from the series *All Things Considered*,[6] the presenter Roy Jenkins interviewed a veteran risk-taker, Canon Andrew White. Canon White is director of the Foundation for Reconciliation in the Middle East, vicar of St George's Anglican Church in Baghdad and a regular visitor to Gaza.

Canon White refers to Baghdad as 'the most dangerous parish in the world'. He explained to Jenkins that the four lay leaders of his church had been killed, and described the successive Sundays when a car bomb went off outside the church then a suicide bomber got into the building. He listed occasions on which he has escaped miraculously with his life: being hijacked and held at gunpoint, escaping shelling in the siege of the Church of the Nativity in Bethlehem, avoiding mortars as he goes about his 'normal work as a vicar'. He also described his relationship with the Iraqi children who have taught him what it means to be entirely defenceless in a war zone.

He told the story of 'The worst dinner party of my life', which was with Saddam Hussein's sons. He attended because to refuse to do so would have meant the death of the Iraqi secret service officer assigned to him.

Asked why he does the job he replied quite simply 'If I don't, nobody else will.' Because there is nobody who has the relationships he has established and who could therefore do what he's doing. He doesn't believe he is indestructible, and he follows the advice of the Foreign Office and embassy – security costs him $2,000 a day. He describes the hope of a peaceful resolution as 'sometimes more theological than political'. But he is convinced that we have to hope.

Asked how his wife and children cope with his lengthy absences from the UK in such a dangerous place, Canon White replied 'My wife has never known me doing anything else and she does not worry about me at all.' He acknowledged that they have to protect their two little boys from the reality of the work that their father does.

Risk may well involve us holding a particular fundamental commitment – even a particular truth – in tension with another. For most of us the risks will not be as stark as those taken by the vicar of Baghdad, but nevertheless they are real.

Risk can be a good thing, leading to a fuller experience of life and to discoveries about ourselves, others and God that would otherwise have remained uncovered. But we are never sure whether we are taking the right risks, so there's often that sense of seeing only one step ahead – perhaps not even that – hesitantly going where it seems we should, and understanding what we might gain and lose only as we gain and lose it. The poet Theodore Roethke tells us 'This shaking keeps me steady, I should know. I learn by going where I have to go.'[7] It is in the very nature of risk that we don't know whether or not it will be worth it.

And so we return to that seminal risk of birth. God knows this precarious human existence from the inside, and in Christ was by no means risk averse. Had that been the case, the Jesus story would have both begun and ended very differently – as it is, it tells the fragile, resilient, angry, courageous reality of what it is to be human.

I should say that Hannah Sophia was delivered safely, that she weighed only 4 lb 6 oz and spent 17 days in special care. And that she's now a long-legged, energetic and spirited five-year-old, whose precarious beginning did not stop us trying, two years later, for a second child.

Of course risks must be weighed and considered in the full knowledge of our connection with others, of the fragility of life itself and of our responsibility to live it wisely. But the nature of life is that the risks are always with us – and that there is everything to gain.

2

Managing without God
The reality of doubt

In the United States presidential election of 2004, George W. Bush was challenged by Senator John F. Kerry. During the days leading up to the election a photograph of Kerry appeared in a number of national newspapers. It showed him standing in front of an illuminated cross, declaiming his message, punching the air for emphasis. It was a picture of certainty, backed by a huge Christian symbol.

For many of us, Christian believing involves just as much doubt as conviction. That doubt takes many different forms. In the sleepless small hours when energy levels are low, when problems loom larger than in the daytime or the literal darkness of the world drains the colour from life, faith can be faint and elusive. As brakes scream behind us on a motorway or a tube train stops in a tunnel for no obvious reason, faith suddenly seems too fragile to face the terror that might come.

In the aftermath of bad news, when the familiar framework of our life is threatened, faith may seem wholly absent. Or when we are intractably out of sorts and we simply don't know why, faith can be the ficklest of friends. Doubt, some would say, is just part of the package of belief. Particularly if the God we believe in is not one who protects us from the daily irritations or the big questions.

'God would have us know that we must live as those who manage our lives without him . . . Before God and with God we live without God.'[1] Dietrich Bonhoeffer offers us an unpalatable truth. It's not that God is unconcerned with the intimate detail of our lives. Rather, that we are given the ability to manage many, many things pretty much on our own, making use of the God-given gifts of experience, sensitivity and reason. God is alongside us always but expects us to get on with the day-to-day stuff like grown-ups. And being grown-up is harder and not always so much fun as we used to think it would be.

Living this way, we will inevitably have our moments of doubt. Far easier to wrap ourselves in the comfort blanket of blind faith, believing that God will smooth every ripple and anaesthetize every minor pain. But grown-up faith means taking on the responsibilities God has given us, and therefore getting it right sometimes, and sometimes messing up. It means being exposed to the harsh realities of life as well as its rich joys. Which in turn means that doubt, at times, will be very real.

We can choose what to do with our doubt. We can deny it, to ourselves and to others, and live the fantasy of an unchallenged faith. But the energy required to do this is considerable. Dishonesty with our self is very draining and is destructive rather than creative. Dishonesty with others undermines our relationships and constrains the growth of our relationship with God. How can we connect with God when we are disconnected from others and ourselves, and when we are suppressing real and essential questions about life?

So the other response to our doubts is to face them head-on, acknowledging their presence, their substance and their power to destabilize us. Acknowledging them leads to hard questions about the meaning and direction of our lives. But the questions are real, and the likelihood of connecting meaningfully with ourselves, with others and with God is far greater if we are prepared to face one another as we truly are, unfettered by pretence.

Once we have decided to work with our doubts, rather than deny them, we discover strands within the traditions of Christian faith that will help us in that struggle.

For the Church, the themes of the Advent season – the weeks immediately prior to Christmas – are charged with chaos, conflict, fear and uncertainty. In Luke's Gospel, Jesus describes how it will be when the time has come for the world as we know it to end: 'There will be signs in the sun, the moon, and the stars, and on the earth distress among nations confused by the roaring of the sea and the waves. People will faint from fear and foreboding of what is coming upon the world, for the powers of the heavens will be shaken.'[2]

Advent raises fundamental questions about where we might look to for our security.

In early December one year, my daughters and I were in the National Gallery, gazing at a glorious painting by Rubens of Samson prostrate in Delilah's lap. 'Is he dead?' asked four-year-old Hannah. 'No, not dead, just asleep,' I said cheerfully. I told her the story, explaining that Samson's physical power was dependent on his hair never being cut, but Delilah had seduced him into a trap and his enemies had shorn Samson's locks, rudely depriving him of his strength.

Hannah was still wrestling with the concept of hair loss equalling loss of strength when her father arrived to meet us. In a stunningly appropriate coincidence he had come via a session at the gym and then a haircut.

For a split second as she took in his short hair, the possibility of a Daddy with no strength shadowed Hannah's face. No more shoulder-rides across the park at breakneck speed or breath-squeezing bear-hugs or easy lifts up onto a carousel horse. Her world would come crashing in without the security of that strong and protecting presence.

And in the same way our world is not the same in the moments, days and even weeks when we seriously doubt the existence of a powerful, nurturing and concerned cosmic parent.

In his book *The Company of Strangers*, Paul Seabright explores the emergence of our economic institutions and how they influence the affairs of the world. He remembers the query of the Russian official responsible for bread production in St Petersburg, two years after the break-up of the Soviet Union. 'We need to understand the fundamental details of how [a market system] works. Tell me, for example: Who is in charge of the supply of bread to the population of London?'[3]

Who is in charge? Is anyone? If so, do their concerns include our needs, our safety, our wellbeing? If the answer, miraculously, is yes, do they actually have the power to make a difference? Or is that primeval hope of an ultimate and powerful something – beyond me yet connected with me – an unhappy illusion? These are the real questions our doubt raises, and that our faith has to face, not hide from.

And often, in response, we receive God's silence. In Saint

Mark's account of Christ's crucifixion we are told: 'The people mocked and shouted, "He saved others, he cannot save himself". And Jesus cried "My God, my God, why hast thou forsaken me?"'[4] They have to be the most desolate words spoken from the cross. And what did God say in response?

Nothing.

Words matter to us. Explanations matter. Many people have raged against God's silence. In moments of grief, despair, bereavement or isolation, we want to do that, and we probably should.

But some have asked: What if God did speak? What could God possibly say that would make all of this alright? We can't imagine anything that could be said to explain away the worst of human pain. And wouldn't God's words, if they were words we could understand, be inevitably limiting?

Denise Levertov's poem 'Immersion' offers an alternative take on God's silence:

. . . God is surely
Patiently trying to immerse us in a different language,
Events of grace, horrifying scrolls of history
And the unearned retrieval of blessings lost for ever,
The poor grass returning after drought, timid, persistent.
God's abstention is only from human dialects. The holy voice
Utters its woe and glory in myriad musics, in signs and
    portents.[5]

We are driven to make sense of things in words. Which, when we think about it, is a risky project, because words can create such distance between people. Words carelessly chosen. Words carefully chosen that can't help but offend because they reach into situations so sore, so fragile, that they are bound to fall short and emphasize the gap between two people.

So perhaps it is good that God's way of communicating is different. That God speaks with us not in open and direct conversation, but through the circumstances of our lives and the events of our world.

We feel exposed by God's silence. It does nothing to reassure us. We fear our own ignorance, our incomprehension, our struggle to compute and process and understand the world.

Yet again, if we can face this fear rather than ignore or deny it, we may give ourselves the space to learn God's other languages. God is not constrained by sound-bites or even a keynote speech. God's message is eternally re-expressed in ways beyond the grasp of human vocabulary, but sometimes within the reach of our other skills and senses.

God is the creator of visual and sensory communication, between ourselves and the physical universe and between ourselves and others. God is the initiator of the conversation between human beings that is not about words but is the intertwining of lives and hopes and aspirations. Some of the most formative experiences that we have of the world and of each other are not experiences of hearing but of seeing. Seeing the sheer physical beauty and precision of the created world. Seeing the richness of other people's gifts, the wholeness of their lives, the colour and grace and dignity of their human being. Our moments of most 'felt' connection with God can come through such seeing.

They can also come through story. We explore other people's stories to help make sense of our own. The stories of friends, of communities, of our workplace; stories we read in novels and newspapers; political, cultural and religious narratives – they are all invaluable tools as we seek to interpret ourselves and the world.

For Christians, the Hebrew and New Testament Scriptures provide a significant and rich wealth of narratives. These stories emerged across centuries in a huge variety of contexts and cultures. The texts are in the form of poetry, myth, letters, wise sayings and what we know as Gospels – attempts by people who had a close connection with him to interpret the life of Jesus.

We set our own stories alongside these and each becomes a differently shaped piece in a complex jigsaw puzzle. Some pieces connect, areas of the picture grow, and partial though it is we discover something of ourselves and of God in the shapes, colours and incomplete images that are revealed.

And then there is the story of incarnation, of 'God in human form'. It tells of God's coming among us in Christ – from the stark physicality of a cold birth in first-century Palestine to the ignominy of crucifixion – and speaks loudly and clearly of God's irreversible entanglement with the world. If stories are a language in themselves, God, the ultimate source of our own narratives, is fluent in this tongue.

So facing our doubts head-on, inevitably frustrated by God's silence, we can at least try to learn God's other languages. There are signs and symbols of God's love embedded here, in the created world of earth, sea, stars and teeming humanity. There is a silence that perhaps frees us by protecting the space in which new things can be expressed and ancient truths be retold in a fresh way. There are the stories of those whose lives are entangled with ours, both now and in human history, and there is the reality of God among us in the particularity of one life. All of these languages help us to reach through our doubts to something real, beyond.

In her deeply thoughtful book, *Things Seen and Unseen*, the American author Nora Gallagher recorded a year lived in a church community. She wrote about doubt:

> I live in a world full of evil. And my faith cannot always endure it. And thus I doubt. Doubt is to me the handmaiden to faith, its cop, the one that keeps faith straight . . . But it is also so easy to doubt, so easy to be cynical, that the job appears to be to enlarge the part that believes, but only to enlarge it by taking the path made painful by the doubt and with the integrity born of the doubt rather than the inflation born of sentiment, heightened emotion, or the sometimes false camaraderie of a faith community . . .[6]

If we're living with a sense of God's silence and absence as well as God's story and presence, it probably means that we're facing reality head-on. We are acutely aware of our own vulnerability and the fragility of others, awake to the fact that God may be closer to us than our very breath, but the act of breathing remains our responsibility.

If we're living like this then the opportunity is there, however painful, to enlarge the part of us that believes, while at the same time refusing to let go of the questions.

The specific ways in which we enlarge our capacity for God will be different for all of us. And for each of us in the different phases of our life.

Exploring God's language of silence may mean honouring our frustration by shouting into the darkness. Or it may mean sitting in that silence, holding our fear of nothingness in our hands, asking that God be alongside us. It may mean identifying what it is that we hope for, if God's silence is truly freeing God to re-create and re-form the world.

Exploring God's other languages may mean enlarging our belief through our love of art or music, of dance, cinema or reading. Through our love of another person. Through our gift for hospitality, creating occasions for others to connect and God to rest in their midst. Through our ability to perceive in complex political situations the mark of God's prompting and presence, or through our commitment to work and all that it offers to ourselves and others. It may be our sensitivity to the changing seasons and an awareness of their inner pulsing life. Through any of these means and so many more we may nurture and grow our sense of the sacred.

For some of us our sense of God's presence is encouraged through the worship and community of a church. I find that when I don't take part in public worship for a long period of time I have more doubts. I re-enter the Christian community and it's like putting on an old, comfortable, warm cardigan – I am held and reassured and uplifted and I know that I believe. And yet para-doxically some of my strongest experiences of God's presence in the world happen in places and with people to whom the struc-tures of the Church are an irrelevance. All of this neither proves nor disproves God's existence or the truth of the Christian story. It just reminds me that I should continue to wrestle with the doubts and the questions about where and how God is to be found.

Yet however many ways we find of enlarging our capacity for God, it may be that none of them lead to certainty – or at least not all of the time.

For many, for now, that has to be enough. In the harshest of situations – when we are facing illness, death, loss, betrayal, dis-appointment – this can seem like far from enough to get through the day. Yet as the film director Bela Tarr once said, it seems to be the case that 'The more desperate we are, the more hope there is.'[7] Humanity has a tremendous capacity to hold on to hope in the direst of circumstances. Perhaps that tenacity is more than reality-avoidance and wishful thinking. Perhaps in moments of desperation we're grasping at a truth and not just a straw.

The photograph of John Kerry standing before a back-lit cross and declaiming his certainty could have been of many other people, confident in their politics or their faith. It was a disconcerting picture because it communicated a message that admitted no room for doubt. Part of what it is to be human, part of what it is to grow, part of what it is to believe, is to be willing to struggle with the hardest questions, to face our own doubts and fear, and to use that experience to enlarge our faith.

One year prior to her encounter with Rubens' Samson and Delilah, Hannah was asked to do a painting herself. She was to design the front page of a carol service sheet. The service was to begin with a poem – quite an abstract poem – and the illustration was supposed to respond to the poem's words. They were good words, and they were quirky words, and they were random, in a way, and in another way connected. And Hannah and I took some paint and some sponges and some brushes, and we had a dialogue – which sometimes connected and sometimes didn't.

And I didn't know whether I understood the poem, and Hannah wasn't in the least bit interested in anything but the paint – she was, after all, just short of her third birthday at the time. Yet somehow God breathed through the words, encouraged the artist and probably wished the mother would butt out – and something was created and made sense and made no sense and was ordered and was chaos, and had darkness, energy and space, and was glorious and full of awe. It said much about Advent and much about our human experience. The fact that it said it obliquely, pictorially and almost accidentally, made it all the more similar to life.

Our doubts and our hope, our anger and our ecstasy, our disturbed sleep and our moments of profound peace, are all places where we can meet with God. Uncertainty is part of the fabric of human being. We need to face and grasp and respond to it as creatively as we can with all the energy we can summon. We may be very unsure exactly where we are in the artist's picture, we may have moments of doubt that the artist even exists, but we enlarge our capacity for God only through our willingness to live with the disorder and the doubts – the awe and the silence.

3

I am 32 people

Understanding our several selves

I am two people;
and one is longing to serve thee utterly, and one is afraid:
O Lord have compassion upon me.
I am two people;
and one will labour to the end, and one is already weary:
O Lord have compassion upon me.
I am two people;
And one knows the suffering of the world, and one knows
  only their own:
O Lord have compassion upon me.[1]

The late Austen Williams, who was vicar of St Martin-in-the-Fields
in Trafalgar Square for 30 years, used this prayer often. When asked
by the current vicar, Nicholas Holtam, whether he wrote it himself, Austen replied appropriately, 'I am not sure.' He went on to
suggest that everything has more than one origin – mirroring the
way that we all have more than one self.

Each time I hear 'I am two people' my first reaction is always,
'Yes, us too!' My second thought is that to be only two people would
be blessedly simple – 32 seems nearer the truth some days.

One reason I remember Austen with fondness is the occasion
when he asked Nicholas, 'Are you still working with that blonde
bombshell?' I'm neither blonde nor that sort of a bombshell, but
my mixture of delight and indignation at the remark cast light on
at least two of the people that I am. The other 30 looked on, amused.

'I no longer know what is real, what is accident, what is inten-
tion. I talk to myself and I am not there. I miss me.'[2] Those words
are from a particularly harrowing episode of the crime detection

drama *Wire in the Blood*. The clinical psychologist himself, suffering from an invasive brain tumour, is temporarily unable to distinguish between what belongs to his actual lived experience and what is only in his head. Because he does not know which bits are real, he's not sure what defines him as himself. As he's the one whose job is to unpack and analyse other people – to strip out the untruth from the truth – it's a particularly harsh irony.

Yet on some level doesn't this experience resonate with all of us? Are any of us ever sure which bits of us are real and which are the habits, protective layers, even virtual 'other selves' that over a lifetime we have created and accumulated?

In the autumn of 2006 the Local Environment minister, Ben Bradshaw, asked the grocery-shopping public to take direct action. Supermarkets, he said, were using an unnecessary amount of packaging. Practices were changing, but not quickly enough to stem the flow of rubbish into Britain's landfill sites. Bradshaw suggested that in order to focus retailers' minds, shoppers should leave excessive wrapping at the tills.

It was a call to arms, an encouragement to rip the bags from the bananas and tear the plastic off those little trays of peaches.

But it's not only supermarkets that need to peel off the packaging. In a less literal sense we all wrap ourselves in multiple layers. Rather than allowing the subtleties and nuances of how we think and feel to be exposed to others, we succumb to the temptation to adopt a stereotype – pulling it on like a winter coat. It's easier, safer, tidier.

At work we may choose to package ourselves as 'omnicompetent colleague, cheerfully juggling an impossible workload'. At the school gate we pray that the mask of eternally cheerful parent has no obvious cracks in it. With friends we are the storyteller, or the cynic, or the quiet one. It's easier to wrap ourselves in the same familiar blanket than to shed those protective layers and simply be ourselves with courage and maturity in any given circumstance.

God surely sees the protective layers in which we cocoon ourselves. And God surely hears when we slip into our other habit of using words as a way of avoiding truth or complexity. In the public realm this is called spin. In the workplace it manifests itself in impenetrable jargon. In personal relationships it's about talking about nothing in order not to communicate anything.

In Zadie Smith's novel *On Beauty*, Claire has always been bemused by the success of the 30-year marriage of her friends, Kiki and Howard. She, being a poet, is puzzled that the relationship has survived when the two of them communicate so differently. 'She called a rose a rose. He called it an accumulation of cultural and biological constructions circulating around the mutually attracting binary poles of nature/artifice.'[3] What Claire does not know is that the marriage is coming apart at the seams, and that from Kiki's perspective Howard is using excessive layers of irrelevant vocabulary in an attempt to barricade himself from the truth.

In the end, our metaphorical layers of garments and unnecessary words only diminish us. They cloud our self-understanding and create barriers between ourselves and others. But it takes courage to allow our more complicated and interesting selves to meet fully with God and with other people. Partly because there is a sense in which, over time, our protective layers really have become part of us. Recognizing which of the layers are unhelpful and trying to peel them away can be very painful.

Of course there is a sense in which we are all, quite legitimately and authentically, more than one person. Or at least we're one person playing numerous roles, and carefully negotiating the overlaps, the inevitable clashes and the uncertain ground in between. At one and the same time we may be the boss, an employee and a colleague. We might be one of the lads chilling out in the bar and later awake in the small hours with the responsibility to care for a sick child. We are a confident party animal and the intimidated newcomer to a group.

We are an adult partner and a needy child. We are enjoying the freedom of a girls' night out, but in the knowledge that tomorrow we have hard decisions to make in the boardroom. At home, in the community, or at work we are responsible, confident and assured – in the surgery or hospital we are surprised to discover that we suffer from white-coat syndrome.

In these and many other contexts and relationships we hide, reveal and explore different aspects of ourselves, discovering that though they may be contradictory they are, in fact, real. For most of us they are at least partly infused with mystery. There will always be bits of ourselves that we don't understand. And bits that don't quite hang together.

But it matters to us that we work creatively with the lifelong puzzle that is our 'self'; that we discover and rediscover at least part of who we are; that we make sense, add up, and are able to define and describe ourselves with some level of coherence. We want to believe that our priorities, loves and commitments are fundamentally compatible; that there is a single thread – or at least some intertwined fibres – connecting the different aspects of ourselves and the many roles that we play.

The poet Kapka Kassabova puts it:

> Waking up in the same skin isn't enough.
> You need more and more evidence
> Of who it is that
> Wakes up in the same skin.[4]

Our habit of packaging ourselves simply and neatly is partly about our own fear of facing the bits of us that we really don't like. Or sometimes it's because we inhabit an environment that discourages us from too much self-revelation. I vividly remember arriving as a young curate in my first parish and being advised that it would probably be better not to tell people that I was separated from my husband and soon to be divorced. The situation was carefully handled and I was treated with great sensitivity. The decision about what to do was ultimately mine. Yet there was a view – grounded of course in reality – that I needed to protect myself from suspicion and criticism.

So I took that advice. There were important parts of my story that I simply didn't tell. For a long time I concealed from many people significant things about myself – things that had formed and shaped me and made me the sort of priest that I am.

A church at its best is a place where people are able to be fully themselves and to hear and know that God embraces them in their complexity and vulnerability. Churches can offer sanctuaries of acceptance where people are simply held, un-judged, in their vulnerability, fears, weakness, regrets and guilt. Such communities encourage people to be honest with themselves and others about the most difficult aspects of their lives as well as the candyfloss and the icing.

This is not to suggest that churches should adopt the flaccid liberalism that believes all behaviours are acceptable and that any choice we make is fine by God. Nor to recommend the sort of inclusion that pretends we are all the same and that human interaction is a breeze provided we hug one another often. Rather, in places where we are able to be truly real to each other, 'Our lives are transformed *because* we overcome the fear, guilt and prejudice . . .'[5]

At its worst, the Church can positively discourage people's ability to be honest about themselves. In the era when most clergy who were gay did not openly acknowledge their sexuality, that defining expression of who they were was not an issue for the Church as a whole. Latterly some gay clergy have spoken and lived in such a way that there is a greater public awareness about who they are. Consequently on many different levels they have experienced the Church as reluctant to tolerate let alone embrace and welcome them. Women clergy, in certain times and places, experience something similar.

So when in November 2006 the Rt Revd Tom Butler, Bishop of Southwark, referred publicly – and in the climate of that time, courageously – to gay and female clergy as 'blessings', the language was somewhat counter-cultural, and a refreshing affirmation of many, many people.[6]

Of course, there are appropriate levels of self-revelation – not everyone needs to know everything about us all of the time. Similarly, we can use our life experiences to shape our work and relationships without needing to wear our hearts on our sleeves. But untold damage is done to individuals when an institution encourages or even demands of its members a lifestyle that requires them to dissemble. It is a costly and dishonest way of trying to create harmonious communities that ultimately fails to achieve its goal.

These issues are not confined to the Church. How much of ourselves we might reveal without being sidelined or ostracized by our colleagues is a difficult issue for many. Sometimes it's a question of how far we can raise our head above the parapet without getting shot, or at least removed from our position so that we can no longer influence anything at all.

For some the question is relevant even closer to home. Do we risk being misunderstood by our family and friends for the sake of greater openness? We can undermine carefully nurtured relationships of trust by telling people more about ourselves than they can handle. Yet peace of mind and personal integrity are significant parts of the equation as well.

In the instances when we decide it must be done, peeling off the layers of our disguise may be painful. Distinguishing between the real and less than authentic versions of ourselves can be a complex process. Opening up our uncertainties to others – and to ourselves – makes us vulnerable to misunderstanding and confusion.

In all of this the rather abstract question 'Who am I?' is not always the most helpful guide. But there might be another approach to examining and refocusing ourselves.

Mark's Gospel presents Jesus as someone who will not tell anyone who he is – at least, not in so many words. Unclean spirits identify him and are told to be silent. People he cures are exhorted not to tell anyone what he's done. And the phrase he uses most often to describe himself is Son of Man – an ambiguity that could mean just anybody or could mean the Messiah.

On Good Friday, Pilate wanted the truth out of Jesus, the truth about who Jesus was. He asks 'Are you the King of the Jews?' and Jesus answers enigmatically, 'You say so.' We knew that already; it gets us no further. But if we look back at the life that led up to that day, it reveals much about what and who Jesus is *for*, which in turn gives a clue to who he is.

Jesus was for healing. He was for the awakening of those he met to the presence of God in themselves and their ordinary experiences. He was for drawing out the miraculous in daily life. He was for the uncovering of a Kingdom where social division was no longer a reality. He was for the inclusion in God's embrace of people of all conditions and habits. He was for acceptance, challenge and love.

He was for everyone. He was for reconnecting people with God. In fact he was so much for that last thing that he *was* God.

We might take our cue from Jesus and concern ourselves less with titles, names and the words that we and others use to identify, define and categorize each other. Perhaps we should sit light to the question 'Who am I?' and be more actively engaged with 'What am I for?'

What am I for, when presented with another person's need? What am I for in the face of the acute poverty that blights a significant proportion of the world's population? What am I for when the demands of paid employment clash directly with the needs and desires of those I love? In all these instances, what I am for helps to form who I am.

An extraordinary book was published in 2004 by the New York columnist Mitch Albom. *The Five People you Meet in Heaven* tells the story of 85-year-old Eddie, who has been a maintenance engineer in a seaside amusement park for most of his life. Within the first pages of the book an accident on a roller-coaster prompts Eddie to throw himself towards a freefalling cart to which a small girl is clinging.

> In those final moments, Eddie seemed to hear the whole world: distant screaming, waves, music . . . his own voice blasting through his chest. The little girl raised her arms. Eddie lunged. His bad leg buckled. He half flew, half stumbled . . . landing on the metal platform, which ripped through his shirt and split open his skin . . . He felt two hands in his own, two small hands. A stunning impact. A blinding flash of light. And then, nothing.[7]

Eddie did not stop to ask who he was – but in that instant he instinctively knew who and what he was for.

We need to peel away the layers of untruth and creatively address our contradictions; to explore the tensions between our different roles. When we don't add up, we sometimes simply need to be held. And through all of this we'd like to discover who we are. It matters to us that our lives have meaning. Asking who and what we are for can help us to discover what that meaning is.

Our meaning is shaped by projects and tasks; by relationships and responsibilities; by successes, disasters, dreams and nightmares. It comes through a passion for the earth, for our work, for the arts. Through learning a new skill or deliberately facing ourselves with a tough challenge. Through our life with others. Through the conviction of religious faith. Or if conviction is too strong a word, through the determination to look to God for our star, for that which orientates us.

In these experiences there are sudden moments of: 'Yes, this is what I'm for, or why I'm here. This is, in fact, part of who I am. It's what I mean.'

And we sometimes learn who we are by stopping. In the stopping we open up space for reflection on what we've done and what we've learnt about ourselves in the process. Sometimes we can reflect in the midst of action, and consciously change and develop and grow as we move on. But space and silence are invaluable too, giving us the opportunity to interpret our reactions, impressions, feelings and perceptions; to perceive the underlying characteristics that compelled us to do what we did, and to do it the way that we did it; to discern what we've become because of all that.

The search for connecting fibres of meaning in our lives is complicated by the fact that we are always changing. Everything that happens to us has an impact of one sort or another, so our self is constantly becoming. We can experience this as either freeing or frightening, or both. Redundancy, retirement, ill health, or the realization that a particular longing that has shaped our life may now never be fulfilled: any of these experiences can lead to painful questions about what our lives have been about and what they are for now.

But in all of this we are held by God. The God who accepts that where we are is the only place from which we can start. The God who, while drawing us on, embraces us unconditionally in each time and place. The God who knows that a fundamental requirement for our growth is our own ability to recognize ourselves as we are, and to believe that that is okay.

In her early weeks at the local primary, which happens to be a Church of England school, our daughter Hannah came home with a scrap of paper on which she had written what she said was her 'Pray to God'.

The prayer said (in translation), 'Thank you God for myself.' If that level of self-acceptance is all she achieves at St Mary's, we will bless that school for its wisdom and nurture.

4

More poetry than prose
The DNA of difference

If death is a great leveller, then so is the Edgware Road. Squeezed on either side by the residential areas of Paddington and Marylebone, it's both an arterial route out of London and a busy local shopping street. Always noisy, always busy, the pavements are populated with students, office workers, business people, babies in buggies – and numerous individuals heading for 'shisha' cafés or beating a path to the Woolworths' sale.

The Chinese woman at the till in the supermarket teases Hannah about the number of jellies we're buying. The owner of a Lebanese café greets us warmly every time we pass by. On the bus both children are restless, and women in burkhas smile, the sympathy unmistakable in their eyes.

Edgware Road is a great leveller because it constantly reminds us that we are part of a great crowd. We hold concerns, joys, needs and habits in common with many other people. This levelling is not oppressive but liberating, because the living, breathing, talking, walking, teeming human melee reminds us that no one, but no one, is the same. We hold many human experiences in common, while being gloriously individual and distinct.

In April 2006 we moved into a red-brick flat on a quietish street just one step back from the crowd. From our second-floor vantage point the girls observed their new neighbours. For several months, each time we ventured out onto our balcony the members of a Middle Eastern family waved from the windows opposite. In August they suddenly disappeared and the flat was closed up. Friends told us that the family spend the winter in Saudi Arabia but would be back the following spring. Across the span of the street we never did discover whether we had a language in common, but the smiles and waves were more than enough to welcome us to the neighbourhood.

And of course there was a language we shared, but it was neither Arabic nor English. We had become linguists of posture and facial expression, visual connection and familiar nods. It was a warm, tentative, respectful language – and fully acknowledging of difference.

The language of difference has more to do with poetry than prose. Prose attempts to tell us, with precision, how things are, setting them out through description and definition. There are implicit limits around the possible ways of interpreting the writer's message. In poetry, the boundaries of meaning are somehow more permeable and there is significant space for the reader to explore. Poetry evokes rather than defines. It communicates by hints and gestures, nuances and symbols, instinct and sensation, so that it's possible for us to make connections that are outside of the poet's own experience.

Of course this is to generalize considerably. Some prose is highly poetic, and some poems are more straightforwardly descriptive than others. But in general terms poetry is the more spacious way of communicating.

I once heard it said that women tend towards a more poetic approach when finding language to talk about God. Men, it was argued, have a preference for prose. This too is a generalization. Some women will not recognize themselves in it and some men will protest that they prefer symbol and metaphor to prosaic explanations. The DNA of difference is always complex and particular. Many general statements about people of a particular gender, ethnicity, age or sexual orientation fall a long way short of capturing the richer and more interesting truth.

So the language of difference is poetry, not prose. We know when we are in the presence of something or someone other than ourselves – but we can't express the distinctions in bullet-point terms. We think that we've learnt something – but we're not sure what it is. We realize that we've offended someone – but we aren't clear why. We sense that we're being changed through the experience – but we don't yet know how. We proceed by feeling our way.

We cannot domesticate diversity. It can't be tamed or fully un-wrapped. If we want to live deliberately – consciously opening our lives to the breadth and depth of the human melting pot and its potential – we need to sit with the discomfort that 'the other' brings.

The theologian Walter Brueggemann writes eloquently about the idea of 'othering'.[1] He suggests that it is a deliberate and active engagement with another person, with God or with part of ourselves that we consider in some way to be a stranger to us.

God's love embraces the stranger who challenges us as well as the people with whom we feel at ease. It embraces the parts of ourselves that through fear, shame or incomprehension we dare not admit to or own. And it is so different, so fresh, that in it we know we are encountering an Other who will lead us into a new understanding of our place in the world.

If we are to learn through what is strange to us as well as through what is familiar, we need the courage to practise this othering. To wrestle with those aspects of ourselves we can't fully pin down, to encounter the people who are strikingly different from ourselves and to face the God whom we don't understand. We need to sit with these others, talk with them, pray with them, rest with them, in the hope that through the process we might slowly grow and change.

For seven years I was privileged to be part of a church community with English, Cantonese and Mandarin-speaking congregations. The English congregation itself gathered people from Africa, the Caribbean, Asia, Australasia, North America and different parts of Europe. It was a place that necessarily took othering seriously. In the millennium year, the Festival of Pentecost was identified as an opportunity for those different congregations to come together. Everybody's linguistic and cultural contributions were honoured in a vibrant church service and an extravaganza of a party. Over time this became an annual event, and a visible exercise in othering.

The biblical story of the first Pentecost tells us that the disciples, gathered in Jerusalem for a Jewish festival, experienced something that enabled them to communicate the good news of God's love in languages other than their own. A sense of God's glory swept through the crowd as the cacophony somehow resounded with God's Spirit. It was as though in tongues of flame and the breath of wind God's presence swept through the crowd, and no one remained untouched.

So at Pentecost we took up the idea that radically different languages and cultures can be a rich melting pot from which God's power and grace emerge. The celebration was characterized by a blaze of colour and a rich feast of sounds. Together we revealed our otherness, trusting that each would be welcomed and embraced. No one said 'This is how we are and this is what we bring' – we simply were what we were and brought what we did. It was poetry, not prose.

But several celebrations later we began to realize that if the fiesta at Pentecost was to mean anything real, it must be more than an annual assault on our cultural senses. It should be fed and underpinned by our ongoing commitment to live with each other through the disagreements and misunderstandings that are a reality in any community. We needed to honour one another in the teeth of misunderstanding as well as in times of easy connection. We had to root out any patronage, imperialism, or thoughtless assumptions about another's identity or belief.

Over time this commitment faced some robust tests. People held widely varying views about many things: global economics, how Christians should approach fair trade, sexuality and sexual relationships, and the question of salvation through other world faiths. Sometimes the differences could be traced along cultural lines. Most often it was not that simple, and people coming from the same geographical place offered divergent perspectives.

Perhaps even more of a challenge for all of us was to discover our own prejudices – or to have others face us with their perception of our bias. We were a multi-ethnic congregation, gathered at the cosmopolitan centre of a world city. It was easy to assume that we were relatively free of latent racism. But when honesty was encouraged in a safe space, people spoke of experiences of prejudice they had endured over the years in that same church community.

False assumptions and disconnections ran in all directions. We began to listen to what was really being said, rather than what we expected to hear from one another. We realized that until we had the courage to look our dissimilarities fully in the face, we wouldn't really change.

I now work in a role concerned with the contribution made to the Church of England by its female clergy. My experience so far has led me to believe that gender difference is also complex and nuanced, and in many ways remains uncharted. We see this in the debate around questions such as: Can we generalize about the characteristics of women as pastors, as chairs of committees, as preachers and as celebrants at the altar? Do female clergy have something in common other than their gender? If so, do we need to say what it is – assuming that we can? Might the culture of the Church change as more women step into senior roles? Would they conceive those roles differently? Do women lead in a different way? All of which are questions asked in other sectors too.

Until women take up full responsibility and have the appropriate authority at all levels within the Church and elsewhere, we will have no definitive answers to these questions. And when that day comes it will be deeply disappointing if the answers we reach are sterile, boundaried and simplistic. The issues are as subtle and mysterious as women and men themselves. The last thing we need in the promised land is a culture that believes we've got everything analysed, labelled and sorted.

But it does seem logical to assume that the Church, which for centuries was shaped and nurtured and carried by male priests, might in some ways look and feel quite other than it does now when the ministry of ordained women is more fully and freely explored. Already the Church is refreshingly other than it was because of the presence of people who are openly gay. Many respond to that change with cries of fragmentation and dissent. But if we can stay with the pain of exploring disparity – disparity that challenges our assumptions about our own identity – the Church might emerge a more wondrous and gentle creature, better equipped to meet people in the nuanced, fertile and complex reality of their lives.

We may even enter more deeply the God who embraces both masculine and feminine being, and the challenging and delightful relationship between the two. If we are made in God's image then difference is somehow somehow found within Godself, and that must be a good and healing and fertile thing.

It was in the context of a Eucharist service that I saw God differently one May evening some years ago. The gospel story of the Ascension tells us something about the Galilean Jesus becoming the heavenly Christ, risen and ascended in glory, gathering all nations to himself. The disciples who witnessed whatever it was that happened to Jesus that day were caught up in a glory that they did not understand. The experience could not be adequately described, grasped or held on to. It simply had to be indwelt. It was poetry.

The music for that Ascension Day Eucharist included movements from David Fanshawe's *African Sanctus* – a piece that uses distinctive African harmonies, rhythms and instruments and incorporates sounds recorded on the African continent. And the priest who hosted us at the Eucharist was Canon Ossie Schwarz, from the South African Diocese of Kimberley and Kuruman.

If poetry proceeds by hints and gestures it can also offer up a blast of pure connection – a 'yes' moment when we know something we've always known, but that has never been 'surfaced' quite so powerfully or distinctly before. Through the simple facts of a black priest at the altar and the sounds of another continent, we saw and heard God differently. The experience echoed with a different internal language, transposed us to a different key, and translated us to a different place. We ascended with Christ to an African heaven in the context of an eighteenth-century Baroque building.

Many of us were also taken to a different place within ourselves, and the African members of the congregation were at ease with themselves and others in a more profound and joy-filled way than we had ever previously known. For our church community the challenge was to hold on to that while remaining individuals with myriad priorities and practices, attitudes and issues – many of which would continue to test our powers of 'othering' for some time to come.

In a very different moment at my desk in the office of the same church, I struggled one day to write a sermon. The conflict in former Yugoslavia was ongoing, Britain was actively engaged through the United Nations, and I needed to ask: 'Where are we in all of this? Where is God?'

It was then that I came across the theologian Miroslav Volf. Out of personal experience while teaching in his native Croatia during the war there, Volf wrote *Exclusion and Embrace: A Theological Exploration of Identity, Otherness and Reconciliation.*[2] The book caused me to think again about difference, and how we handle it.

I had always assumed that to connect with one another at all we must first discover what we have in common. I now came to believe that true human connection lies in creating the space in which others can be wholly different, then being willing to stay with that difference and to embrace one another in it. It's about really hearing the story of the other – no matter how fearful that makes us, no matter what that other tells us about our world and how it is for them, no matter what painful self-truths we uncover in the process.

Volf gave me the language to address a previous formative experience. Back in 1992, I had sat at a small wooden desk in an ante-room of a mosque in Blackburn. A short distance away was my colleague Laura, who like me faced a long queue of people waiting to tell their stories. We were solicitors' clerks in our mid-twenties, and we had just gained 50 families as new clients. These people were part of the first wave of Bosnian Muslims fleeing the conflict in the Balkans. Arriving in Britain via horrendous lorry journeys, they gravitated to cities such as Blackburn, which had a sizeable Muslim population.

There, in spite of language issues and marked differences in the practice of their faith, they were met with hospitality by the local British Asian Muslims. For legal advice their hosts brought the refugees to us. So we sat and listened to stories of violence, loss, rape and neighbourly betrayal. And in that sparsely furnished room we simply gave space for those stories to be told. At that stage in the process we knew it was all we could do.

We connected through nothing but our raw and uncomprehending humanity. We made no attempt to interpret the experiences that were being described, or to pretend that we knew how it was to be those people in that time and place. We simply marked, recorded and held what they told us, wondering at the tenacity of the human spirit in the face of unspeakable inhumanity.

We were changed. To this day I would find it hard to describe in what way. But for me it was something to do with meeting those who had witnessed the most terrible otherness in the people who had been their neighbours; being shown that the unspeakable does happen.

Where people of difference live alongside one another, or meet, or even just cross each other's paths, they can experience one another as a threat. This is real, and in a primal sense it comes from that knowledge deep in us that the other – the other in others and the other in ourselves – can do unspeakable things to us. Perhaps it is also a fear of what the unknown God might do.

So although the cultural melee is what I love about where I live, I'm aware of being surrounded by people I neither know nor immediately understand. There can be a feeling of being a stranger in a place you consider to be home. The diversity excites but also disturbs. But staying with the discomfort gives immeasurable opportunities to learn and to grow.

Real-life difference – as opposed to the saccharine and neatly packaged version in our heads – can unseat us. It may force us to acknowledge that we neither know nor understand things that we had assumed we had neatly catalogued and taped.

We encounter someone entirely and unremittingly at variance with us; or who is like us in many ways but actually comes from a very different place. The assumptions of our upbringing, our peer group, the dominant culture in which we live, are invaded and overturned. We are suddenly up against prejudices we were not aware we held – about people's priorities, the way they conduct relationships, the politics they take as read or the appropriate way of behaving in particular circumstances.

We learn fast that there are many ways of saying and doing and being and believing, and that we are familiar with only a tiny part of the picture. The real lessons to be learnt are not easy, obvious or superficial, but subtle, nuanced and complex. And they are lessons about us, as well as them. The 'other' in them can bring us hard up against the 'other' in us.

If we are unable to trust to the goodness of the other, as well as to take account of their capacity to hurt us – if, that is to say, we cannot cope with the difference of our neighbours – how will we face the much less easily grasped difference of God? We are made in God's image, yet God is profoundly Other. We need to take the material of our daily lives and embrace the dissimilar in all of it, celebrating the endless shades of its vibrant colours and allowing space for it to remain other.

We won't be sure of being understood, nor that we have understood others. There will be much more poetry than prose. And that will be the beauty of it.

5

My parallel lives

Attempting a creative response to envy

In a passage from her first novel, *Oranges are Not the Only Fruit*, Jeanette Winterson explores the idea that it is possible for one person to live several parallel lives.[1] She suggests that each time we make a choice between two paths, we leave part of our self behind. That part continues along the route we would have taken had we made the alternative choice, and as an expression of some aspect of our self it has substance and a momentum of its own. It's a very attractive idea: most of us find it hard to let go of what else might have been possible, had we lived and chosen differently.

As a variation on this theme, a friend has a theory that we all need at least three lives: one in which to concentrate on our work, one in which to have a partner and children, and one (here I paraphrase) solely dedicated to our pleasurable exploration of the world.

But we don't have three lives. We have one. And therein lies the problem of envy.

To envy is to want something that another person *has* that we don't have, or to want to be what another person *is* that we are not.

There are days when I feel that I am something of an expert on envy. It's arguable that working for the Church of England doesn't help. Although we are getting better at it, the institution has done little until relatively recently to mitigate envy among the clergy. A suspicion of overt ambition coupled with a flat hierarchy, an historically opaque system of preferment and a lack of regard for an individual's need to be stretched and fulfilled have combined to fan the flames. One writer states:

The Anglican church is an example of an organisation that wastes the ego-energy of the individuals within it . . . Many priests . . . recognise a need to play down their ambitions . . . Their egos operate with stealth and caution to get their needs met . . .[2]

So in my professional context I'm dangerously exposed to the possibilities of envy. But my expertise extends to the private and much more personal sphere too. For example, I'm no longer shocked by the theory I once read that the mothers of teenage girls envy their daughters' figures, hair and unquenchable youthful vibe. In fact I've arrived a decade early, wishing I had my five-year-old's legs-up-to-her-armpits and my three-year-old's feather-soft skin. And I envy some other women the quality of their fat – yes, the quality. No longer does it seem worthwhile craving a sylph-like figure, but fat of the non-cellulite variety is so much more attractive than the more developed sort.

Less superficially, I envy my daughter's reception-class teacher her refreshingly relaxed air of competence. I envy the acute political mind of Kirsty Wark and the effortless sensuality and domestic ease of Nigella Lawson. I envy the parents at the school gate who know everybody else at the school gate. And I envy all thirty-something working mothers who have ascended inexorably through the ranks of their profession while absorbing the finer points of parenting, the basics of good leadership and the fashion sense of Kate Moss.

In all of this I've come to the view that envy is generally at its most acute and difficult to handle when it is envy of someone who is roughly our age and with whom we have something in common. So I have particular issues with the thirty-something working mothers because the comparisons are more direct and my excuses for not having achieved what they've achieved run aground.

In the Christian tradition envy is one of the seven deadly sins. The online encyclopedia Wikipedia sagely notes that this is because 'envious people ignore their own blessings, and focus on others' status rather than their own spiritual growth'. Envy diverts our attention to things that don't matter. It stunts our growth. It causes us to squander the God-given gift of our own life.

Wikipedia also informs us that the philosopher Kant distinguished between malignant and benign envy. Envy is malignant if it involves hostility towards others – and particularly the desire for them not to have what they have. Envy of this sort undermines our relationships, preventing us from appreciating, enjoying and learning from others. It works against God's plan that we should love and nurture one another. Rather it adds to the sum total of hostility among human beings.

Kant thought that if envy does not involve hostility then it is benign. But so-called 'benign' envy can also be very damaging to ourselves and to those around us. It wastes time and energy, deflecting us from happier and more nourishing concerns. It erects a barrier between ourselves and the God who wants to encourage us into a full expression of our own being – not watch us attempt to be somebody else.

Ultimately, envy pushes us out of shape. While desiring something other than what we have and are, we thwart God's longing for us to grow more fully, wholly and wonderfully into ourselves, and instead become what we certainly never intended to be: bitter, disappointed, rather sad, and disconnected from our Creator and those who love us for what we are.

In November 2005, an article appeared on the BBC website that began: 'BBC Radio 4 would like the men of Birmingham to answer this question: What is Missing from Your Life?' Some of the responses received were woven into a drama-documentary by the writer Stephanie Dale.[3] These included mention of World Cup tickets, sports cars, more noughts at the end of a bank balance, and olive farms in Tuscany. But there were also recurring themes that related to 'home'. Men spoke of wanting to be at home in their own lives, longing for a place they could really call home, and needing to belong properly.

We have a fundamental human need for belonging and a deep desire to be comfortable in our own skin. Even if we accept the creative possibilities of risk, we usually need a level of self-confidence and some degree of security before we have the courage to embrace anything unknown.

To be comfortable in our own skin and to feel that we belong in the world, we need to deal with our envy and address its underlying longings. Otherwise our peace of mind will be disturbed by a troubling restlessness and dissatisfaction. So how might we tackle envy creatively?

I return to the conviction that we cannot truly learn, grow or live deliberately unless we are prepared to be honest. That honesty extends beyond ourselves to honesty before God. It might even – so far as wisdom permits – prompt some brave conversations with others. Unearthing and frankly acknowledging our envies is a prerequisite to doing something positive with them.

Once the need for honesty is accepted the following could be three ways of taking the process further. The first involves separating the longings that are real, God-given and creative from those that are unreal, arise from less helpful sources and are a waste of energy. The second is about working with the reality of our boundaries – both challenging what appears to be non-choice, and accepting that our supposed limitations might liberate us to connect with God's grace in new ways. The third is about rejoicing in our interdependence and recognizing the unique nature of our own gifts and of God's work in and through us. Together these approaches might encourage us to inhabit our own lives more fully, rather than trying to appropriate aspects of other people's.

First, the attempt to separate the real longings from the unreal. It is a truism – but no less true for that – to say that some of us are fortunate enough to be confused about what we want because there are so many options open to us. From our vantage point in the West and the global North, what we know of the world reveals countless attractive possibilities. We have only to scan the television listings to see a little of what is on offer. You can be discovered overnight and get your longed-for break in the West End. You can persuade wealthy entrepreneurs to invest significant amounts of their money in your dream project. You can escape the urban nightmare to build a new life in the country. You can flee the British countryside to discover an entirely different pace of living in Andalusia.

These options, schemes, plans and dreams – and the many others waved before us – appeal to different aspects of our selves. But are they really the goals to which we want to commit most of our time, energy and long-term focus? Do they appeal to our deepest hopes, aspirations and motives?

I was privileged some time ago to hear Rebecca Stephens, the first British woman to climb Everest and the Seven Summits, speaking about her experiences. Before her presentation I read a short account of Rebecca's life to date and had more than a fleeting sense of 'Why have I not achieved so much with my life?' Unfortunately, the age gap was insufficient to deal neatly with the question, and so I arrived at the seminar expecting to spend an hour feeling dissatisfied with myself.

Listening to Rebecca's account of risking her life in sub-zero conditions, digging snow-holes in order to survive nights of unprecedented storms, painfully summoning the strength to take even one step at high altitude and reaching the top of one peak only to vomit with exhaustion, I had a revelation: while admiring the woman greatly, I had no desire to have done what she's done or be who she is!

We need to take a long, hard look at what we envy and ask whether it truly resonates with the fundamental priorities and concerns of our lives; whether it connects with what we discern to be our God-given strengths; whether it would help us to grow in the areas in which we have felt God challenging us.

The second approach to envy is to identify the real boundaries around our aspirations. There will be some limits imposed by external circumstances that we cannot change. Depending on what these are, acceptance without resentment can be a lifelong struggle.

A friend in her forties who has lived long-term with a debilitating and only partly diagnosed medical condition sometimes astounds me with text messages that speak with genuine delight of small triumphs and happinesses in her daily life. At times she is singularly appreciative of life within what others would consider unbearable constraints. Pushing the boundaries that she can, and living within those that she cannot, she finds God in a very narrowly defined space. Glimpsing signs of life in the garden, managing to get out of the house for an hour or being able to help a friend in emotional turmoil are all ways in which Fiona discovers and takes part in the life of God.

The inevitable result of some boundaries is loss and pain, frustration and anger at the limitations imposed. No one can tell someone else how to live within and with such painful circumstances. But when people do it with such courage, those of us with less constraints are reminded of our responsibility to test the boundaries we assume to be ours.

For some of us there will be boundaries that it is within our power to shift, because when we face them honestly we have to acknowledge that they are self-imposed. We may have constructed them through fear of failure. Or we may have accepted without question what others show or tell us is 'the only way' to do things. What other people model can have a significant impact. In assuming that we can only do things as they do, we capitulate unnecessarily to what may be imagined limitations. There will be ways in which we can achieve the same or similar things differently. The risk might well be worth taking.

In professional terms my own albeit privileged decision to 'work more flexibly' in order to spend time at home with two children felt very risky. I was afraid of disappearing off the church's radar after giving it ten years of my working life. Here on the other side of that decision I marvel at the unforeseen opportunities it has opened up, the new discoveries it has made possible, the excitement and learning it has led to and the aspects of that same institution it has enabled me to engage with differently.

Sometimes the very things that appear to limit our horizons broaden them considerably in another sense. Or perhaps a better metaphor would be that they enable us to drill down where we would otherwise have not, and to discover the God who permeates all things.

An article appeared in the *Guardian* some time ago by Kirsty Gunn. The introductory paragraph ran 'Kirsty Gunn is not working on her next novel. She is not a columnist for the *London Review of Books*. She has chosen instead to disappear from the professional world and embrace a domestic life just as rich and interesting and inspiring . . .'[4]

Gunn's poem, 'Sweeping up Stars', reflects on an afternoon spent with her children playing with glitter, glue and paint. Getting out the dustpan and brush, she muses that the occasions on which she will do this again are limited, wondering exactly how often she will have the opportunity:

> To gather in
> The bits of glitter, sweep up brightness

From the floor, to tip into the bin
Bright constellations . . . How much time
To sweep up stars?[5]

Boundaries that are set by geography, employment, retirement or a responsibility to care for others often have the potential to open up new spaces within ourselves and in our relationship with creation and other people. They can speak to us of worlds within worlds – worlds of love and connection, beauty and meaning that we previously failed to see. Living wakefully and deliberately within our particular boundaries, we can all have our moments of 'sweeping up stars', those moments when, if we look at it for long enough and in a certain way, the fundamental stuff of life connects with the divine.

The third approach to a creative relationship with envy is to appreciate the possibilities of interdependence. In 2006, I attended a programme offered by the Windsor Leadership Trust. The Trust brings together individuals who would never usually meet because they are drawn from such a wide range of organizations. The combination of high quality input and the time to reflect and share insights about leadership results in some significant pieces of learning.

Attending the programme at a time in my life when I was giving up a recognized leadership role and taking on a much less defined professional identity, I read the information about the other participants with a sense of impending doom. Each had achieved so much in their lives to date, both within and outside of the context of work. They had positioned themselves impressively within their organization, while in their spare time managing to stretch themselves considerably through, for example, their sailing, microlighting and skydiving activities (not a word of a lie).

Small wonder that I approached the course with some trepidation. But it didn't take long for somebody to admit that they felt exactly the same as I did – then someone else, then someone else. In an atmosphere of extraordinary trust and honesty among virtual strangers, what ought to have been obvious soon became wholly apparent – that we all have our fair share of self-doubt, struggle and questioning; that no one has anything like all the answers to all of the questions; and that together we are far better placed to address the issues facing us than we ever will be alone.

And for me another truth emerged: that each individual has a unique combination of experiences, relationships and opportunities that enables them to achieve certain very specific things. I felt the force of this when I heard a priest talk about the things that her particular experience uniquely placed her to do, and her conviction that she must do them because no one else can.

So one antidote to envy is to accept that you are your own unique and singular self. You are the only person who can reflect God in the world in precisely the way that you are positioned to do. The interconnection of lives, circumstances, events and happenings that makes you truly what you are is yours alone. God can act in and through you in a way that God cannot act in and through anyone else.

Dealing with envy has something to do with finding a home in ourselves. We need to inhabit our own life, not somebody else's. It's about finding God in the detail of our own day, not our colleague's or a friend's. It involves recognizing that, with very few exceptions, we all envy one another in some way at some time.

So to return to the beginning and Jeanette Winterson's theory, my parallel lives are fairly numerous. There is the human rights lawyer I never became, the archdeacon I'm highly unlikely to become, and the bestselling author who remains but a distant illusion.

Then there are the smaller projects I will probably now only ever experience through others. There will always be the part of me that wishes I had worked the 'six months in a refugee camp for VSO' that I sort of promised my grandfather in exchange for him funding my first ball-gown. And the bit that wishes I had been more physically adventurous and bungee-jumped from that bridge over Victoria Falls. 'Learn to play the cello' will probably remain on my 'to do' list long after the joints in my fingers are past it. And those contemporaries residing in bishops' palaces may well provoke a twinge of envy if and when I reach my dotage.

But the larger part of my heart, mind and soul knows that envy is an empty and unhappy companion, to be met with a robust rebuke; that some of the things we think we long for we don't actually want at all; that many of our boundaries are self-imposed, and some of the real ones can encourage us into a deeper experience of things that really matter; and that in real life we each have our own share of successes, failures, doubts, certainties, delights, sorrows and 'grass is greener' delusions.

We need one another in order to live to the full – and God lives to the full only when the divine is reflected, differently, in each and every one of us.

6

The road not entirely right
The dangers of mere perfectionism

In 1906, the economist Vilfredo Pareto observed that 20 per cent of the population of Italy owned 80 per cent of the country's wealth. He developed a theory that later became known as Pareto's law and has since been adapted to numerous contexts. It now appears in various guises in business management and self-help books, often called the 80:20 rule.

One version of the 80:20 rule says that in relation to any given project, 80 per cent of what is achieved comes from 20 per cent of the effort put in. So once you've delivered 80 per cent of a task, or completed it to 80 per cent satisfaction, it isn't worth much more of your time. Those extra hours or minutes spent wrestling with whatever it is that you're wrestling with will not make a significant difference.

On this analysis, perfectionists waste a lot of time and energy. So if you are one of those people who can't send a text message with imperfect punctuation or an e-mail without a heading you may need to join me in perfectionist rehab. Rehabilitation, sorry.

Our perfectionism can distract us from the main point or from the bigger picture. It can lead us to some unhelpfully harsh judgements when we or others fall short. It can have a 'rabbit in the headlights' effect as the fear of failure prevents us from making any move at all.

Our own insistence on perfection can impact badly on other people's development. A manager's inappropriate micromanagement can quash creativity and innovation. Parents can thwart the early learning curve if they suggest several fundamental improvements to the latest offering of artwork or the misspelt greetings card.

Of course, the fine detail matters a great deal in some contexts and we need those who are willing to engage with it. If we have to undergo neurosurgery the knowledge that our consultant is a perfectionist is likely to be a comfort. Perfectionism can drive us to punch above our weight and achieve beyond our natural capacity. And if someone can manage and use their perfectionist tendencies well, both they and others may grow through the process.

Perfectionism is a double-edged sword.

Across the first draft of this chapter (which in common with this last was far from perfect) I wrote in red ink: 'Be ye perfect – deal with it!', a reference to the Gospel of Matthew and Jesus' words, 'Be perfect, therefore, as your heavenly Father is perfect.'[1]

Any attempt to argue that perfectionism is not all it's cracked up to be needs to address these rather challenging words. Taken at face value they set us an impossible goal. If we are being called to the perfection that we generally assume is found in God, that which is without fault, we know that we are never going to attain it.

But according to my trusted biblical commentary, the verse in question brings together two Hebrew texts, one of which has the word 'blameless' instead of 'perfect', and the other of which uses 'holy'. Luke's version says 'merciful'. The commentary also points out that *teleios*, the Greek word that Matthew uses, is rare in the Gospels. The only other occasion when it appears is in the story of the rich young ruler. Jesus tells him, 'If you would be perfect'. And *teleios* can also mean complete and mature.[2]

This seems to be going in the general direction of something rather less clinical and unattainable than perfection, towards something to do with wholeness, completion and grace. So is God in the business of perfection as we commonly understand it, or is there something rather more interesting going on?

Certainly one popular understanding of creation, the cross and our relationship with God, is built around the idea of perfection. This version assumes that at each stage of the creative act God knew exactly what to do and how to do it. That the 'i's of creation are dotted and the 't's crossed, and that the blueprint for human living is pretty much available online – though tough to put into practice.

This is the sort of theology that wraps things up very neatly. The story it tells of the crucifixion is akin to the resolving of an equation. Things were supposed to be perfect, but humanity messed that up. The consequence is an experience of separation from the Creator. God is grieved, and in Christ, on the cross, takes the consequences for our sin. This somehow rights the equation and God and humanity are reconciled. We can be forgiven for continually messing up because in some cosmic sense Christ has balanced things – made them perfect once again – and in the end this cannot be reversed.

From this understanding of the nature of things comes the assumption that there is always a best way of doing things, an ideal place to be, a perfect picture to paint – then a range of other possibilities stretching through various less than perfect scenarios to utter disaster. If this is how we frame our lives, we judge ourselves on our ability to recognize, achieve, maintain and polish the ideal, while remaining cool and in control, dancing on the pinhead of right decision-making. Anything else feels like failure. Granted, Christ has dealt with that failure, but the way we construct our lives remains an attempt to attain an ideal – to get as close to perfection as we can.

And of course we continually miss the target because we make mistakes. We fail. We fall short.

Our daughters' first nursery school had a blessedly refreshing approach to naughtiness. Their unswerving policy was never to tell children that they were naughty. Instead, the staff used the language of 'good choices and bad choices'. Hence 'Hitting Micah with that plastic dinosaur was a bad choice, Kirsty.' This approach means that Kirsty is not pigeonholed as a naughty child. She therefore does not feel the need to live up to that challenge and isn't pushed into a corner where she might be inclined to give up on herself at an early age. But she is absolutely clear that the decision she made was not a very good one.

Bad choices. We all make them. Wrong turnings we have to reverse out of, or that cause us to take another turn, and another, until we're back on the original road. But not of course at the point we left it. Or wrong turnings that lead us somewhere else altogether. After some seat-of-the-pants navigation we feel that we've got ourselves onto a good track again, but it's certainly not the route we set out intending to take.

Louis MacNeice's poem 'Entirely' debunks the idea that we can ever get anything completely right, remember anything perfectly or find our happiness wholly in one place. He concludes that, 'in brute reality there is no/Road that is right entirely'.[3]

With MacNeice, I believe that there is no journey executed to perfection, no life lived without any sense of 'Maybe that wasn't so wise', no road that is right entirely. And I wonder anyway whether the word 'entire' doesn't suggest a much richer approach to life than that which is constrained by an obsession with what I'm beginning to think of as 'mere' perfection. Perfection speaks to me rather dryly of a lack of mistakes. Entirety suggests something more whole and altogether more embracing. Something that reaches beyond what we might have imagined we could experience or attain. Something that connects with other things rather than stands alone and isolated in its faultlessness.

There is another version of creation's story, the meaning of the cross and the nature of our relationship with God. And I think it has much less to do with perfection and much more to do with entirety. It is eloquently and powerfully described by W. H. Vanstone in *Love's Endeavour, Love's Expense*, and I borrow his terms unashamedly as I have none of my own adequate to say what he's saying.

Vanstone suggests that the act of creation is much more exploratory, risky and precarious than the version where 'i's are dotted and 't's are crossed. In fact at any one point the outcome of God's creativity might as easily be tragedy as triumph.[4] This is because creation is both an artistic endeavour of unprecedented originality and an act of self-giving love. The alternative would be a universe limited by what the creator already comprehended and held static by a love that controls, rather than a project that extended the imagination even of the Creator, and yet left space for created beings to make their own response.

The possibility of triumph or tragedy is integral to courageous artistic expression. And tragedy or triumph are equally possible outcomes of the sort of love that does not seek to control. An artistic work might 'come right' or come wrong.[5] This love might find its fulfilment or be rejected.

Vanstone suggests that because love, by definition, does not wilfully control, there are moments when the creator's control is 'jeopardised and lost' – and evil is a consequence.[6] Yet in such moments the artist's reach is extended beyond previous imaginings as the 'mistake' is worked into the picture and the canvas is won back through creative genius.[7] When it seems that all has been unreservedly given, love finds in itself yet more to give, or as Vanstone puts it, 'through the challenge of the tragic [love discovers within itself] the power which was not there before – the power of yet further endeavour to win back and redeem that which was going astray'.[8] The bottom line is that the Creator will never abandon us but will always work to make things come right.

In this scheme the cross becomes what happens to real, vulnerable, authentic love when it is misunderstood, feared and not recognized for what it is. It is both a statement and an event that points beyond itself to the tragic possibility of love's outcome. And it is part of the attempt 'to win back and redeem that which was going astray',[9] the toughest and most radical and most entire attempt, expressing all of God's desire and longing to win us and the canvas back.

Then Easter Day is the triumph. It is what happens when love is fully given and fully received. Life is wholly and entirely restored. Both Good Friday and Easter Day set out before us fundamental truths about what is possible and real in a world created in an act that is risky, vulnerable and self-emptying.

So I'm not sure that the meaning of the cross is simply an equation to be grasped. It seems rather to be the culmination of a life lived fully, thoughtfully and unreservedly. It is something to do with the suffering of the world and of individuals, with triumph and tragedy, and with sacrifice and self-giving. It is everything to do with God's ultimate refusal to give up on the creation, which is the highest possible expression of the divine artistry and love. The cross is about living entirely because it is a refusal to duck the consequences of the way that the world is.

Where does this leave us in our relationship with the Creator? Perhaps God is like the father who once told me that home is the place where his daughters should be able to have their sulks, strops and tantrums without fear of judgement or reprisal. They need to be held, not judged, as they learn to live with and understand themselves. They are as they are for myriad complex reasons, both within and outside their control. If they can't be this way and work through it safely at home, where and when can they learn to come right, rather than come wrong?

It is in this sense that God is our home. Offering space for us to respond to the love that gives all, always. Knowing that there are imperfections – even glaring mistakes – in the canvas of our lives. Acknowledging that this has as much to do with the nature of God's own creative act as with our response. Determining to remain alongside us as we find ways to paint in our wrong choices as part of the picture that one day will be entire.

People have asked me whether I regret the failure of my first marriage. I regret the hurt it inevitably drew us into. But regret has always seemed an inappropriate word in relation to the wrong choices involved. It seems irrelevant to regret decisions made for the best of reasons, in good faith, according to our understanding and on the information available at the time. The 'givens' of our lives and characters were what they were, and although mistakes were made it was not through carelessness or ill intent.

Growing up is often associated with setting aside particular, childish behaviours, with shedding the things it is no longer acceptable for us to do, be or have. Perhaps the more positive approach is to talk about growing into oneself and one's life more fully and more entirely, working with the artist to explore the full possibilities of the canvas and the paint according to the divine creativity and our response. Not berating ourselves for what, in us, falls short, rather recognizing it as one issue of the precarious nature of the creative act – the reality of the possibility of tragedy – and finding ways of working it in.

There is an oblique but insistent resonance here with the controversy around size zero models. In some kind of warped version of the epithet 'less is more', the quest for the perfect body has become the quest for less and less flesh. Whether the fashion industry has created this problem by promoting the particular look, or is simply giving the fashion-pursuing public something to aspire to and demand, the fact is that models are getting thinner. And they are not the only ones, as smaller-sized clothes are being bought on the high street.

In 2007, a former presenter of *The Clothes Show*, Louise Redknapp, made a documentary on this issue.[10] One of the most moving sequences was the visit to an institution for children with eating disorders. One teenager spoke of waking up every day longing to be another person with another life. At a stage when everything should have been opening up for her it was all closing down. For someone suffering from anorexia, the desire seems to be quite literally to become less. The 'more' that the person is, the greater the self-loathing. Being perfect starts to have some dreadful connection with being nothing. Sufferers commonly speak of a desire to disappear; the perfectionism of 'less, less, less' rather than the entirety of more.

This is an extreme example of where the pursuit of a very specific form of perfectionism might lead us. But there may be in it a salutary warning that perfectionism can lead to a sanitized, neutralized, reduced experience of life and what it is that we are created to be. There are many scenarios where mere perfectionism can stultify and reduce rather than inspire and increase. The gospel themes of wholeness, healing, growth, asking, offering, sharing and connecting all draw us into a broader and deeper experience of God, others and ourselves. God is surely not a reductionist, but a God who meets and holds us entirely.

Someone who lives entirely avoids avoidance. They have an eye to the indirect consequences of their actions as well as the success or otherwise of the specifics they are trying to achieve. Someone who lives entirely might at one time be concerned with a lack of balance in their life, and at another give themselves passionately to something at the cost of something else, because it's so compelling and true. Someone who lives entirely loves without attempting to control and risks for the sake of what might be discovered. Someone who lives entirely accepts that there is no road that is entirely right.

In describing the downsides of perfectionism, a friend uses the analogy of crossing a river. The perfectionist uses stepping-stones and concentrates exclusively on managing to land in the middle of each one, with no near misses, without ever teetering, and certainly never getting their feet wet.

Unfortunately this means that they can't afford to lift their gaze from the next stone – they don't look to left or right. And so the experience of the river-crossing is limited to the view of the stone immediately in front. There is no wider context – it's a reductionist approach to life, whereas surely the task is to keep faith with the general direction, to be moved, astonished, comforted, seduced, inspired by the landscape, and to enjoy the interweaving of our own paths with the footfall of others.

I speak as a recovering perfectionist, but I do believe that perfectionism pursued unremittingly is a rather sterile concept. It is sterile when it obsesses with the precise calibration of errors, the post mortem of another's shortcomings, the mental anguish about why we fell short. It is sterile when it fails to learn from its own mistakes the obvious lesson that mistakes will always be made. It is sterile when its focus is the exhausting effort to come up to scratch next time, rather than to explore what we have become as a result of the mistakes we have made, and how we might do things differently and more fully now.

On the other hand, if perfectionism is about working for things to come right, wanting to add value, fulfil potential, use creative and artistic gifts to the full, it is a very fertile and 'entire' thing.

Our road might not be entirely right but it is entirely the road that we must take, because in our search for wholeness, entirety and an understanding of the bigger picture, we must live a life, and this is the one we find ourselves living. These are our relationships. These are our responsibilities. These are our creations and passions. This is our artistic endeavour. These are the people we love.

And perhaps in all of this we will discover that God too is in the business, not of the sort of perfectionism that merely reduces, stultifies and minimizes into nothing, but rather the sort of entirety that is about relationship and discovery, risk and sacrifice, vulnerability and fragility, encounter and depth. The sort that from a cross says 'I am with you in all of this and more', and means it entirely.

7

A green spiral tattoo
Fertility redefined

My friend has a green spiral tattoo. Spirals can be traced both inwards and outwards – inwards to their very centre, speaking of depth, source and beginning, and outwards for as long as we care to follow them, suggesting eternity, continuity and growth.

My friend with the spiral tattoo is one of the most fertile people I know. She is a gifted artist in a wide range of media – paint, fabric and sculpture among others. She enriches people's lives with her knowledge of good literature. She nurtures a wide range of friendships. And she has a quickened, instinctive spirituality that connects with her lived experience.

The spiral was painted to celebrate 20 years free from cancer – it whirls around a radiotherapy scar positioned above my friend's left ovary. While saving her life, the treatment ended any possibility of her conceiving a child. Yet that tattoo is an icon to living deliberately, signifying that her life is intrinsically fertile.

There are innumerable ways in which human beings explore their fertility. As a student I was privileged to know two members of a religious community who lectured in the theology department. They were extraordinarily well-educated people. It was as though their commitment to a life of celibacy lent a particular edge and zest to their creativity in other areas. They had what seemed to me a remarkable knowledge of art, architecture, history and music as well as philosophy and theology.

That knowledge was shared generously with others, and not just for the sake of imparting information. In art, each painting was understood for what it said about a particular strand in the history of human thought. In music, each piece was offered as a way of connecting with something embedded in ourselves, which in turn spoke of the world in which we live.

They also made great spaghetti bolognese and had a good supply of red wine, which enriched the hospitality they so generously offered their students.

I remain convinced to this day that the energy those men devoted to music, art and their understanding of human nature had a particular force and clarity because they were sexually celibate. I mean no disrespect when I say that their fertility seemed to have been diverted from biological reproduction to other deeply satisfying experiences of sight, sound, taste and touch. And a wide range of people reaped the benefits.

My friend with the spiral tattoo, no children and a fertile life, speaks of the need to leave something behind when she dies – something that will in a sense be a continuation of herself. In most of us this is an innate and compelling desire, and for those who procreate it is neatly taken care of on one level at least – though many may long to leave other footprints too.

People who through circumstance or choice don't have children create alternative legacies. Some effect social change that imprints positively on other people's lives and has an impact well beyond their own. I've known such people challenge and nurture communities, serve charitable trusts, fundraise for key social projects, make voluntary organizations more effective and create new organizations to meet emerging needs.

Others who are single, celibate or in families without children of their own, find creative ways to nurture other people's children. Observing gay friends who pay real and committed attention to their nephews, nieces and others, my own efforts to engage with the lives of my godchildren seem comparatively pitiful!

None of this is to suggest that the entire creative capacity of individuals who are parents is consumed in having children, leaving them without an ounce of altruism, imagination or artistry. Nor that those without children are obliged either to connect with other people's, or to find an artistic or charitable outlet for their energies. It is simply to say that people are fertile in myriad different ways. We spend a lifetime working out what that means for us in our own particular circumstances.

Whatever our creative possibility we need to take it and run with it, whether it means turning a white canvas into a thing of beauty or creating space for people to put their lives back together, being an alternative role model to other people's children or preparing the perfect roast dinner. These things express our resourcefulness and our imagination – our capacity to make and nourish and shape and nurture. What we do with our creativity reflects who we are, where we come from and where we would like to go.

And this has everything to do with God.

The Anglican chaplain of the London College of Fashion says that the creative talents of the students she works among reflect the divine creativity. She sees her job as encouraging people to make that connection for themselves.[1] And she speaks from the solid and exuberant foundation of Jewish and Christian tradition.

From the creation stories onwards, these faiths celebrate a God of abundance and originality, who wills that something should exist out of nothing, then works in partnership with humanity to tend and nourish and luxuriate in the vital 'something' that has emerged.

So in Eden the woman and man are charged with naming and caring for the creatures of the earth.[2] In the desert, Yahweh's followers are given enough to satisfy their needs.[3] In good times, when there is not enough of the earth's harvest to go round, it is because the co-stewards of creation are failing in their role. They must ensure that those who have less are provided for, allowing them to glean the corners of the fields[4] and letting the land lie fallow every seventh year to ensure continued healthy yields.[5] And twice their joy and gratitude to an abundant Creator is expressed through the construction of a temple, gathering the most beautiful and cherished of materials and building them into a celebration of the loveliness of God.[6]

The theme of God as an exuberant, even irrepressible, artist creator, gets an unexpected airing in the biblical story of Job. Job has experienced one personal disaster after another, and has no explanation for any of it. After three friends have tried to comfort him with their blunt-edged theologies of suffering, he shouts to the skies for an explanation.

And at last God responds to Job's demand – but not with an abject 'I'm terribly sorry, yes that is all very unreasonable – I'm sure we can do something about it.' Rather, God responds with an exhilarating manifesto for the triumph of life over not-life, the possibility of something over nothing, the implied hope that ultimately it is the force of creativity and not destruction that will hold sway.

None of which removes an iota of Job's pain, or explains why God created a world in which such suffering is possible. It simply sets Job's immediate experience in the context of another truth, a truth to which the fecund earth bears concrete witness. The story is wonderfully explored in Gustavo Gutiérrez's *On Job: God-Talk and the Suffering of the Innocent.*[7]

Our own need to make, to invent, to reproduce and create echoes the nature of the planet we inhabit. The earth has a seemingly irrepressible desire to offer up life – life that, once in existence, is tenacious. We see this in miniature when dandelions push their way through cracks in the pavement or saplings bend to avoid being broken by the wind. We see it on a grander scale when nature adapts to changing climatic and environmental conditions. We see it in biological terms when a burn begins to heal and the skin is renewed, a damaged liver regenerates itself or a baby born prematurely thrives against the odds.

As individuals we explore our creativity in different ways. Each of us has different themes that trigger our response to God as creator and source of all things. Some see God in the intricacy of the tiniest detail of a flower head. Others in the powerful surge of a Cornish tide. Others in the grandeur of the Scottish Highlands. Still others in a sweeping cityscape. There can be something of a rural–urban split here, but many see God's creativity in both arenas – in human ingenuity and the natural world.

Edmund Newell, Canon Chancellor of St Paul's Cathedral, explored this idea in a sunrise radio broadcast on Easter Day 2007. Looking out at the vista from the top of the dome of the cathedral, he spoke eloquently of the intensity of cities, their ability to kick-start our adrenaline, and the excitement and expectancy they elicit. He also spoke of the very different landscape of Exmoor, which was the backdrop to his childhood, and how the expanse of such a place can 'truly speak of God's grandeur and instil an inner peace'.[8]

Both experiences resonate for me. I was brought up a mile from the Lancashire–Yorkshire border, in the shadow of the Pennines –

to be clear, on the Lancashire side – and the landscapes that provided the backdrop to my childhood were the Brontës' Yorkshire moors and the hills made famous by the Lancashire witches. Visitors often see those hills as windswept and the moors as bleak, but I've never been able to breathe that air without a sense of taking in something of God.

When we connect with our sense of what is above and beyond ourselves and also intimately present in the rocks and earth on which we stand, our own capacity to think and act with imagination is released. The fresh emptiness of fells and moorland connects me with the God who creates for the sake of creating, to honour the glory of simply being, to celebrate space and freedom, and not simply to offer houseroom to humanity.

Yet my spirit is equally quickened by the city. Arriving back at Euston station from visits to the north there's that unmistakable frisson of re-entering a fecund mass of humanity. It's a profoundly physical experience and it speaks of the unstoppable energy of human endeavour, the irrepressible urge to decide and act and make and achieve. It offers diversity of choice and endless potential connections. It's intoxicating, and to be handled with care. But it connects me with the same God of the fells, though in a very different guise!

As we explore the connections between God's creativity and our own, we become more practised at asking which paths are life-affirming and which will lead to a deadening of our fertility and the undermining of our connection with God. So we apply the 'Is this life-giving or not?' litmus test to our relationships, the use of our resources and time, the jobs we apply for, the way we nurture our children and many other fundamental issues.

But we don't terminate all relationships that are less than inspiring and all activities that threaten to send us to sleep – though there may be times when that's the right thing to do. More often, we look for ways to turn a deadening situation into one that might give life. We can't always second-guess the outcome of our decisions. We can only weigh the different creative possibilities of each alternative. Yet living honestly and deliberately means doing this as consistently as we can, gradually learning to distinguish what enhances life from the things that diminish it.

Observing children as they create and explore, I notice some general tendencies. They are at their most inventive when they believe in themselves, when they push the boundaries and when they have a questioning or playful approach to any instructions they have been given. They respond to gentle guidance but switch off when someone tries to control or constrain their creative decisions. They are at their most imaginative when they understand that what they are creating does not need to be a replica of something that already exists.

Adults seem pretty much the same, though the stakes are higher and the desire to be told what to do can easily creep in. Choices about creative living are hard when the buck stops with the one who makes them. They become infinitely more complex when played out on a global scale.

In the ongoing debate about our global environment, we are making tough and multi-disciplinary decisions. We now know that the human community has presumed too heavily on the gratuitous nature of creation, taken for granted the eternal fertility of the earth, and become complacent in the relationship with its many blessings.

In *Bursting at the Seams*, the 2007 Reith Lectures, the economist Jeffrey Sachs characterized the world as 'extraordinarily crowded' – bursting in human, ecological and economic terms.[9] If the analysis is right, the gratuitous life described in the book of Job is now threatened in a way unprecedented in human history.

Among those threats are our own excessive demands on finite energy sources, our desire for more and more consumables, our pollution of the planet's water supplies and our prodigious production of carbon emissions. The casualties, to name a few, are those people living in dire poverty, those continuing to suffer from diseases for which cures have long been available and those whose lives are shaped by the travesty of war – war being intimately connected with the inequitable distribution of resources. The challenge, Sachs argued, is for the human community to find ways to co-operate globally in the absence of a global government, to find ways of accessing the expertise held in 'epistemic communities' – communities of specialist knowledge – that might hold the solutions to the global problems that we face, to find ways of living peaceably and through peace find solutions to such issues.

If at the heart of what it means to be human is an irrepressible urge to create rather than destroy, then with Sachs we can be hopeful that solutions will be found. This will involve a sustained effort to stem the tide and reverse the flow of the damage, and to work more consistently with, rather than against, the earth's capacity for evolution and healing.

In Barbara Kingsolver's short story 'Blueprints', a young science teacher is positive about the future of the planet, if not of the human race. Lydia suggests that the reason we are here now is that we are adapted for survival. If we blew it, something better adapted would remain. 'It all started with the blue-green algae, and if humans blew themselves off the map it would start all over again. Blue-green algae had been found growing on the inside of the nuclear reactors at San Onofre.'[10]

A version of this argument made an appearance over a Sunday lunch with friends some time ago. The general consensus was that we must do what we can to minimize our own carbon footprint, and that human beings are responsible for a significant amount of damage to the environment, but also that the world is in a continual state of flux, adapting to forces we are unaware of and don't understand, as well as those we all too culpably know about. And whether or not humanity figures as part of the world's mid-term future, that evolution will continue.

This could be mistaken for complacency. To me it is a salutary reminder of the life within the life of the world, and the imperative to connect with that life in a way that is responsible, aware, and takes account of the future as well as the present, and others as well as ourselves. When we interact with the fabric of the world we are engaging with the life of God in a very specific and particular way. The odds are high – what we do affects the physical reality of which we are a part and that reality comes from God. But the chances are good, too, of connecting with the life that initiates, forms and sustains the created world.

Continued debates in the areas of assisted fertility and embryo research highlight our need to take ourselves seriously as co-stewards with God of the life of creation. As science makes possible greater precision and choice in the processes that lead to enhanced fertility, the responsibilities grow. From questions around genetic engineering and stem-cell research, to the issue of selective terminations to avoid multiple births, the field is crowded with difficult ethical decisions for which, by definition, there is no precedent.

Religious groups that protest against any experimentation in this area seem to do so on the grounds that this is God's arena, and not to be trespassed on by human beings. Perhaps the most overused phrase in the debate is the injunction that 'We must not play God'. But we share with God in the cultivation and stewardship of the rest of creation, and accept our responsibility for that. At what point do we decide that the creative process is no longer our business?

Of course there are some incredibly nuanced issues to grapple with, and the potential for the worst of bad decisions to be made. There are those who hold diametrically opposed views, and many who are ranged in between. But in all of this there is the tremendous potential to encounter God through the miracle of the possibility of life at all. And the opportunity to work with the divine impulse towards wholeness, for instance through processes that might lead to healing for those who suffer from debilitating disease.

There are increasingly complex questions here about what is life-giving and what is life-denying. But the greatest travesty, surely, would be not to ask, 'Where might this take us?' for fear of not being able to answer the corresponding question, 'Where *should* we go?'

Questions of fertility are complex and emotive in the public arena, and demanding and nuanced in our own lives. There are probably creative moments we need to capture before their potential is lost. There may be other times when we must simply hold our nerve until the life-giving path becomes clearer.

My friend has a green spiral tattoo. The spiral whirls around a radiotherapy scar positioned above her left ovary. While saving her life, the treatment ended any possibility of the conception of a child. The spiral is a symbol of a fertile life, lived deliberately.

Depending on which way we follow it at any one time, the spiral that traces our relationship with God and the world takes us into ourselves and the depth and source of our being, or out into the world where we also meet the one who gives life.

Fertility of all kinds is something of a mystery. It can be encouraged and nurtured but it is certainly not at our beck and call. There are many ways to be fertile. My friend with the spiral tattoo and no children is one of the most fertile people I know.

8

The ordinary magic
God's glory in small graces

My nephew's name is Ben. He was born on All Saints Day in 2000 to delighted parents and a very excited big sister called Megan. The family grapevine worked rapidly and we all rejoiced at the safe arrival of our newest miracle. Then just a few hours later it was discovered that Ben has Down's Syndrome. For everyone concerned, delight was immediately dovetailed with anxious questions about his health and future, questions that for a long time were urgent and unanswered.

At the age of seven months Ben had major heart surgery and in the years that have followed his family have taken him to countless hospital appointments and learnt all that they can about his developmental needs. They have ensured that he has access to the most appropriate schooling, filled in endless forms for his Disability Living Allowance, and among all this found time to promote the work of the Down's Syndrome Association.

In common with most other households with children, they have also watched nativity plays, explored playgrounds, acquired an impressive collection of children's DVDs, hosted ambitious birthday parties, visited Legoland and towed a caravan to family holidays in the four corners of Britain and beyond.

People who care for someone who has a disability or is ill long-term, say that part of the experience is about appreciating the small graces in life. Those moments of humour, connection and hope that those of us who don't have to pay such close attention to the basics fail to relish, or even to notice.

Soon after his birth I mentioned Ben to an American woman called Thea, who for a short time attended St Martin-in-the-Fields. I barely knew her, but was touched by her openness to life and to

God. Connections with complete strangers – even such brief connections – can form and change us if we are fully present to them.
After Thea returned to the United States a parcel arrived through
the post. Opening it I found a remarkable book by Martha Beck
called *Expecting Adam*.

Martha and her husband John were Harvard academics with
very specific goals when they discovered that she was pregnant with
a son who had Down's Syndrome. In a moving and forthright
account, Martha opens up some of what Adam has taught her,
including the miracle of the small, seemingly ordinary details of
life. She writes, '[Adam] is constantly reminding me that real magic
doesn't come from achieving the perfect appearance, from being
Cinderella at the ball with both glass slippers and a killer hair-
style. The real magic is in the pumpkin, in the mice, in the moon-
light; not beyond ordinary life, but within it.'[1]

The world is shot through with glimpses of God's glory. They
are often put before us in simple ways, in conversation, in our observation of other people's lives, in our waking dreams, in our perceptions of what is going on in the wider world. If we want the
real magic, we need to notice the signs and symbols of God's
love which are embedded here, in the reality of the world that
we inhabit. We need to develop particular habits and powers of
observation and engagement.

But we're not always too good at paying attention to small things.
The fine details and gifts of our daily life often pass unnoticed
because our head is in another place. We're too distracted by issues
we assume are more urgent or important. Or perhaps we feel
foolish for hoping that there's meaning in life beyond that which
we construct for ourselves.

In T. S. Eliot's 'The Love Song of J. Alfred Prufrock' the narrator speaks of measuring out his life 'with coffee spoons'[2] while
failing to speak, in the ordinariness of a moment 'among the porce-
lain,'[3] of the profound questions that occur to him. The poem is
sprinkled with evocative references to 'sunsets', 'silent seas', 'bare
arms' and 'soft October nights' – small things pointing Prufrock
beyond the surface to the life within life. But he hasn't the
courage to speak of the possibility of that life, because he knows
he may be misunderstood or may misunderstand someone else.
Fearing to upset the balance of his own world, he keeps quiet,

never quite engaging with what is stirring insistently below the surface.

In the most difficult of situations people find hints of God's presence, and sometimes through the small, the ordinary and the mundane. In eleven years as a priest I've heard stories of loneliness, pain and fear from people whose sense of God in all things somehow remains, and for the most tenuous of reasons.

For others, of course, it does not. For most of us faith is pretty precarious, and in moments of despair can be clung on to, sadly relinquished, rediscovered, angrily rejected or fallen upon for the first time. One thing it can't be is explained. What triggers belief rather than unbelief is so often unexpected, obscure, bizarre or mundane.

'People tell me terrible things over coffee,'[4] muses the Scottish poet Kathy Galloway, in a poem that speaks about the dilemma of how to respond when an ordinary conversation turns into an extraordinary human revelation. Through the simple fact of an encounter between two people – one with something to say, one with the ability to hear – realities previously unspoken are suddenly there, on the table, to be respected, taken up and held.

But often we're too focused on our own issues to give someone the space to speak of theirs, too distracted by a bigger project – which could wait, actually – or even just too busy to be at the table at all. Paying attention to the small things easily goes by the board.

Such attention – or the lack of it – is the theme that lies at the heart of Jesus' parable about the wise and foolish bridesmaids.[5] The story is based on the Palestinian custom for the bridegroom to fetch his bride from her parents' house and take her to his own. So the bridesmaids in the story were sitting up with her, into the night, as she waited for the groom to arrive. He was late. As they waited their lamps burned against the darkness. Half had brought extra oil in case the wait was longer than anticipated. The others had not, and their lamps eventually went out.

I always wonder what those bridesmaids might have talked about – had Jesus chosen to tease out the story – before they became drowsy and slept. In the untold version did they share their own aspirations to marry and have a family, or their hopes of avoiding all that and living differently from their friend? Did they reassure her that they would still be there for her in her new life? Did they ask her what small things they might do to ease her adjustment into a new family? Did they tell her how much they loved her?

Or were half of them, at least, as carelessly unaware of the hopes and fears, the longings and insecurities, the intimacies and nuances of the moment as they were of the need to bring extra oil? Were they immune to the beauty of the Mediterranean night? Did they squander the potential of that unexpected oasis of time spent with friends?

Sometimes, perhaps we are like them – in our practical disarray, in our reluctance to connect emotionally, in our failure to draw out the meaning of the moment.

The story of the ten bridesmaids is set very firmly in a series of parables about the coming of the end of the world – which is in fact a beginning. Jesus speaks of a time when nations will wage war against one another, people will betray those whom they love, the sun will be darkened, the stars will fall from heaven, one person will be taken and another left and the Son of Man will come.

Then we have these stories of people who were not ready when the moment came. Jesus talks in no uncertain terms about the consequences of that un-readiness. The slave in charge of the household who is found eating and drinking with the drunkards is cut into pieces and put with the hypocrites.[6] The man who buried his one talent is thrown into outer darkness.[7] Those who failed to visit the stranger in prison and to clothe the naked are sent to eternal punishment.[8]

And the door of the wedding feast is cruelly shut against those whose negligence has allowed their lamps to go out. 'Later the other bridesmaids came also, saying, "Lord, Lord, open to us". But he replied, "Truly I tell you, I do not know you". Keep awake therefore, for you know neither the day nor the hour.'[9]

If we believe it is in God's nature to exclude people from the divine love and presence, then the meaning of the parable is simple and clear. Make bad decisions now, attach ourselves to the wrong priorities, fail to repent before our time runs out, be caught unprepared, and the condemnation is final.

If our understanding of God's love is that it is unreservedly gracious and embracing, we will search for a different meaning.

And we may find the strong and salutary message that life is not to be trifled with even in its smallest details.

It matters what we pay attention to. It matters how prepared we are in our day to day living, even in the little things. Perhaps especially in the little things, partly because they matter in themselves, and partly because how we deal with them has an impact on what else we can attend to.

Our neglect has as much impact as our care, and that can be hard on those around us. We know this to be true. We have all failed to notice another's small but insistent need. We've all missed out on moments, opportunities, connections because we've been too busy looking for the next interesting project. We have all been guilty of that absent presence that fails our colleagues, friends or family because our attention is on other things that at the time seem more urgent – or just more exciting.

God's life breaks into our everyday existence in the form of questions such as: What are you doing with your time and why? Are you really listening to that person? Are you noticing those you love or taking them for granted? What sort of attention are you paying to what sort of things? Are you glimpsing God in those momentary flashes of glory we are sometimes given in the colours of our ordinary day?

Reminders of God's presence are to be found in the here and now and the today of our life. The hints and gestures of my todays include shafts of late afternoon sunlight warming the floorboards of our living room, a book that brings unexpected understanding, a fit of unstoppable giggles shared with my mother, London plane trees, the instant when a sentence suddenly comes right, a saxophone played well, my daughter delighting in her new-found ability to tease me, and the pelicans in St James's Park.

And of course many people will say these are simply experiences of being human in a created world, none of this having anything to do with God. And I have no answer to that, other than to say I believe that they have. And that for me, being human and inhabiting that world is everything to do with God.

In her poem 'The Way We Live', Kathleen Jamie asks for a tambourine in order that she might 'bash out praises' to the God of – among other things – chicken tandoori, airports, mountains, giros, launderettes and dreaming waitresses.[10] She is speaking about the images forever imprinted on a person's mind, stored away, never lost. We all have them, so that over a lifetime we become a collection of vivid memories of all that we noticed and were drawn to and all that gets our blood racing. All this we might connect with in order to discover the pulsing life in life. This is the stuff that is apart from us and yet part of us, in which we can catch glimpses of the colour and texture and otherness of God.

If our sensitivity to the so-called ordinary is not switched on, we pass over beauty and radiance. We miss out on the sudden transformation of our day by a thing of nature or artifice that might have reflected God's glory. We neglect the connections with other people that can be the path to new understanding and a deeper sense of what it means to be human. And we just don't notice the God of small things.

In the BBC radio series *Cities Without Maps*, the journalist and broadcaster Tim Gardam visited a Methodist church above a bookshop in the heart of Liverpool. The church is called 'Somewhere Else' and by all accounts is some*thing* else as well. It is a community that explores a radically alternative approach to 'being church', an approach that is gathering people who otherwise would probably not connect with church at all, many of whom understand themselves as being on the margins of mainstream society.

The church's physical home is essentially a large kitchen, which contains industrial ovens and a sink. People are invited to come and make bread – the invitation is as simple as that. The minister of 'the bread church', Barbara Glasson, speaks with conviction of 'the transforming power of the small'.[11] It's about taking one simple act, doing it in one place, and gathering a relatively small group of people at any one time. In the unselfconscious ease and intimacy of this place, people gather, the bread rises and lives unfold in the warmth.

In the bread church there is a prayer room 'at the end of the corridor'. Some use it, some don't. But in the simple actions of mixing, kneading, shaping, waiting, baking, cooling, eating and giving, all are bringing and discovering things about themselves, each other and God.[12] Through the sharing of small, ordinary actions, what really matters emerges.

It matters what we do with God's love, in relation to the little things as well as the big. We might think that our influence on the world is minimal – that what we do and say has only limited reverberations. But actually our days are made up of myriad decisions about whether or not we choose to notice other people, how we nurture or damage those for whom we have a responsibility to care, what we do to the creation with which we interact, how we pray about the complex issues of violence and broken community that pervade the news, whether or not we smile at the woman we buy our newspaper from or the stranger who walks into our office or church.

It all matters. And what we judge to be the most insignificant gestures can make the biggest difference to other people. In Christ we take on the responsibility to nurture gentleness, truth and grace consistently in ourselves and others, in the small things as well as in the big, in order that we and others may be gripped by God's love, and God might be more fully revealed in us all.

Alan Hollinghurst's novel *The Line of Beauty* is a story of sexual exploration, wealth, beauty, human connection and meaning. Set in Margaret Thatcher's Britain, the story is primarily of a young man called Nick. Towards the end of the book his lover is dying of AIDS and he himself is awaiting the result of an HIV test. He feels profoundly exiled, having lost or been alienated from almost all those he has loved. In the final moments of the story it comes to Nick with conviction that the result of his HIV test will be positive. He is overcome by a terrifying and compelling sense of connection with the world.

> The fear was inside himself but the world around him, the parked cars, the cruising taxi, the church spire among the trees, had also been changed. They had been revealed . . . The emotion was startling . . . He looked in bewilderment at number 24, the final house with its regalia of stucco swags and bows. It wasn't just this street corner but the fact of a street corner at all that seemed, in the light of the moment, so beautiful.[13]

We may recognize this. The juxtaposition of futility and meaning, alienation and connection, exile and a profound sense of being at home in the world. The terror of vulnerable and fragile lives.

The miracle of small things when everything is under threat. All of this is real and many of us will connect with it.

The novel gets its title from something called an 'ogee'. An ogee is a line akin to a double curve, originating in Middle Eastern architecture. It is a kind of guiding principle in design, a measure against which beauty might be set. It has about it a sense of heaven – of something with an origin beyond our immediate perception.

We know the line of beauty when we see it in the physical structures and natural phenomena around us, as perhaps we know the signs of heaven when we perceive them in the so-called ordinary things of life. Because contrary to the popular saying, it may well be the divine that is in the detail.

9

The faint hope of Sabbath
Surviving the culture of fatigue

Nobody has enough time. Enough time for what? Time to see friends, to go to the gym, to have a haircut. Time to spend with our partner, to learn to play the piano, to speak Mandarin Chinese or to go to a Test match. Time to cut the grass, time to clean the kids' shoes. Time for a long walk, time just to chill.

The world has contracted and if we're one of the lucky ones our opportunities have increased exponentially. There's so much to learn, experience, do and be. But mostly, we don't think we have the time.

A friend recently secured a sought-after job in a market-leading consultancy firm. One of the things she likes most about the company is that 'everyone has done something outside of work'. They've run a marathon or two, climbed Kilimanjaro or gained their private pilot's licence. They mentor schoolchildren or act with local drama groups.

We reminded my friend that she's no exception to this rule. She learnt to play the mandolin specifically to perform one piece on a single occasion in Westminster Cathedral!

The book of Exodus tells us that 'the Lord blessed the Sabbath day and consecrated it'.[1] If something is consecrated it goes from being an ordinary thing to a thing that points to the extraordinary and is therefore no longer ordinary in itself. When the priest consecrates bread at the Eucharist, we see it as a sign of something heavenly, holy and extraordinary. It signifies something beyond its own being – the miracle and reality of God made flesh in the material of the same world of which we are part. We then see the significance – even the sacredness – in the bread itself. It is the very stuff of life, nourishing and sustaining us, and therefore connects us with the God who gives us everything that we have.

So when God consecrated a supposedly ordinary day, that day became a pointer to the significance of all days. In its very set-apart-ness the Sabbath signified that all days are holy, because all days are created by God. God blessed the Sabbath, in order to signpost the God-given and God-filled nature of the entire week.

Some people successfully find Sabbath in the midst of incredibly busy and pressurized lives. By Sabbath I mean a time of rest, blessing and insight. But when I talk about Sabbath rest, I don't necessarily mean the sort of rest that in our mind's eye has its most idyllic form in a hammock slung between two palm trees over a white-sand beach. I mean rest in the sense of doing something different or differently in order to recognize that all of life is extraordinary and sacred.

So Sabbath may mean doing something other than wading through endless piles of washing. Something other than battling with an ever-filling inbox. Something other than listening to the problems and issues and conundrums of other people. Something other than writing lists of things to do.

Or it may mean doing the usual things but with a different approach. If Sabbath is about recognizing God in all that is, then the whole of life has Sabbath potential. Not the sort that feels like a short break or a year out, but the sort that sustains us in our daily living.

We might expectantly turn to the Church to school us in the ways of the Sabbath. We might also be disappointed. The Church can sometimes, and not unfairly, be caricatured as a place that doles out tasks – responsibility for the children's work, the church-warden's brief, the role of stewardship campaign co-ordinator, hospitality provider, worship leader. Church becomes a more demanding environment than work.

And to crown it all it offers the clergy who – with a few notable exceptions – in turn model the over-stretched, short-of-sleep and juggling-too-many-plates way of being. Not that we are any more overworked than a chef doing unsociable shifts, a city worker clocking up 20-hour days or a social worker with an unmanageable caseload. The clergy do not have a monopoly on unhealthy working practice and burnout. But we and the Church sometimes fail in our responsibility to signpost an alternative, more Sabbath-conscious way of being.

Simon Parke, author of *The Beautiful Life: Ten New Commandments because Life Could Be Better*, once wrote a pithy column in the *Church Times* debunking the singularly unhelpful phrase 'work-life balance'. Parke cited the argument that no one, in their final moments, wishes they'd spent more time in the office. He then responded rather provocatively, 'many will not be wishing they'd spent a little longer with their families, either – or in church. Successive surveys reveal that people receive as much – or even more – satisfaction from work as they do from families or communities.'[2]

Some of us won't identify with that but some will. And similarly, with Parke's subsequent suggestion that the problem with the whole 'work-life' concept is that it falsely separates the two into different arenas. He suggests that on one level everything we do is work, because all our activities require effort. Most significantly, the effort to be present in the moment, rather than dreaming about the future or mulling over the past.

This imperative to live in the present moment rather than being mentally elsewhere is one of the keys to Sabbath. Sabbath should help us to be fully present, because it points us to what is within the moment and the present task, and encourages us to stay with that.

Even when the word 'work' is understood in its commonly used sense, it can be that thing that points us to the sacredness of all life. It can inspire us, ask the best of us, demand of us that we become more than we currently are – simply because we can, or because what we could be would enhance the lives of others. Work can be a place where human beings come together in supportive and creative relationships, building something worthwhile. People have some of their best ideas at work. Work at its best is life-giving.

As I write, the trend in more forward-looking organizations is to encourage fertile connections between work and life. This is about seeing the workplace as somewhere to which we can bring gifts, passions and skills picked up elsewhere, and use them in a way that both energizes us and contributes to our working environment. Equally it's about seeing the workplace as somewhere that can offer the resources to develop who we are beyond the specific task in hand. And then to allow our new abilities and gifts to spill over into the rest of our lives.

For organizations and individuals this approach holds promise of a greater wholeness of being. It's a welcome alternative to the 24/7 working culture. A colleague dubbed it the 10:10 approach – referring to verse 10 of chapter 10 of John's Gospel: 'I came that they may have life, and have it abundantly.'

As organizations and as individuals there are practical ways to encourage ourselves in our search for Sabbath. When we take something up, we might let something else go. When we have a particularly busy period looming over the horizon, we might take out of the diary things that are non-essential. When home is particularly demanding, we might allow ourselves the luxury of not going the extra several miles at work, and vice versa. All of these things we could probably do without the sky falling in. But mostly we don't!

As clergy at St Martin-in-the-Fields, one attempt to increase Sabbath in our working lives took the form of scheduling a staff meeting with no agenda several times a year. Predictably this began as a 'blue sky meeting'. But that set an expectation that new ideas and projects would be born of it – and they were! So we converted some of the blue skies to 'white space': a place and time set apart to get beyond the blue sky and sit, quietly and thoughtfully, with the help of Scripture and silence, prayer and contemplation, in the atmosphere that would remind us why we were there at all, why we were engaged in these projects and tasks, why we believed in God and perhaps even why we believed in Sabbath.

There's a lot to be said for just stopping. In his novel *Be Near Me*, Andrew O'Hagan writes 'the search for happiness is all we have. To sit in a park and listen to the dogs barking; to sit in a park and hear church bells: are we not always present, always human and always religious according to our faith?'[3] We are gloriously human when we are able to be truly present, and in those moments we are connected with the things of God – perhaps whether or not we would describe the experience in those terms.

Yet we find it terribly difficult to stop. A common cry among my husband's male friends is, 'We get to the end of the day and she just can't sit down and chill. She has to be doing things all the time.' But of course that's not a character trait only 'she' possesses. We all have an issue with that fourth commandment. It's just so hard to stop. But from its context I would say God intended the command as a blessing, not a test. If we could see the truth of our haggard, short-tempered, less than fresh-faced selves more often, we might be inspired to get better at stopping. But we just don't look hard at ourselves terribly often.

And we do have a habit of finding 'quick-fix Sabbaths', which work on one level but don't permeate to where we really need the change. These quick fixes fall into two categories: the ones that are harmless and the ones that, potentially, are not.

The relatively harmless ones might be the serial evenings in front of the television watching trash in order to unwind – or the after-noons when we put the children there for longer than might be good for them in order to gain some peace!

A more insidious false Sabbath might be that habit of relying on several drinks most evenings as our de-stressing routine. A friend points out that,

> Just as one can do Sabbath alone or with people, one can do alcohol alone or with people; alcohol is a depressant, a quietening – the party effect coming from the quietening of inhibitions. I have to acknowledge in my own life a powerful false Sabbath of those 2.5 pints (there's a decimal point in there!) consumed quietly on my own at the end of a stressed day.

We can think that we're finding Sabbath when that's not what it is at all. Or conversely, we can find Sabbath moments in places we'd never have expected.

I was surprised to find myself in EuroDisney one Easter. Having no parish commitments meant that to be there at that time was possible, and somehow in the fine balance of family life it became desirable. I was even more surprised to find myself contemplating the image of Disneyland Paris as eternal Sabbath! Because it is a place that makes you stop and look, a place where there is relaxation and laughter, gentleness and joy, an attentive-ness to small detail and a fundamental belief that hopes and dreams, ideas and fantasies, can be transforming. I won't push the allusion too hard. It doesn't hold much further! But it was an unexpected experience of grace.

We impoverish the idea of Sabbath if it becomes simply a synonym for 'weekend'. Sabbath can mean finding space within all that we do to actually notice what we're doing. It can mean approaching work in a different and perhaps more reverent way, seeing in it the seeds of holiness. A golden thread of Sabbath can be woven through all our activity, so that we don't have to wait for 10 p.m., or Sunday, or our fortnight in Tuscany or Center Parcs before we experience the 'hammock' factor and rest in the present moment.

Anyone who has ever worked with me – or lived with me – will tell you that I'm much better at talking about Sabbath than I am at living it. But there's a longing in me that I haven't given up on pursuing, a longing for spaciousness and the quality of rest that leads to regeneration, a longing for more blue sky and white space, a longing to connect, in a moment where all activity is suspended, with what is above and beyond and through all that we are and do and long for.

So in the context of worship I often want less talking and more silence. And I wonder, when we continually generate noise, what we are running away from. God's spaciousness? Our own emptiness? Running is one option. But staying can push us to listen hard to what is within us, and to gain direction and a greater sense of self and meaning.

In a sense we are pared down without our activity. It's difficult to imagine 'being' without 'doing', or to define where the two are distinct. But if the only way we can live with that question about our own meaning and purpose is to drown its insistent voice in noise and activity, how do we know that the 'doing' is the right doing? How do we know that it arises from the source that will enable us to become our fullest and most authentic selves?

I sense in myself and others a new mysticism – which is as old as the hills, and only feels new because the current assumption is that another and very different version is the 'ideal'. Mysticism is the belief that there is meaning in life[4] and that it comes from God; that God is real, that the reality of God permeates humanity and the created world; and that there's an immediacy with which God can be experienced in the world.[5]

This new–old mysticism refuses to believe that God can only be fully experienced when we have swept the chessboard of our life clean of all its pieces – or at least set them aside for some time. The new mysticism rejects the idea that in order to contemplate life we must in some sense stop it happening, step out of it, create oceans of silence and space.

Of course, the space and silence approach will always be a very attractive way to go for those who find it even remotely possible. And a measure of it will be lapped up by the new mystics in hard-won, more spacious moments, because we certainly do long for it. But mostly the immediacy of our connection with God will be in and through our activity, relationships, tasks and engagements with the world.

I am weary of aspiring to an impossible 'ideal' of finding regular and sizeable rafts of time simply to 'hold my life before God'. The monastic model is wonderfully engaged with the world, and I have no desire to dishonour it. But it doesn't connect with my life and I can't achieve anything that resembles it even faintly.

My life is populated with prams and plasters, chapters and broadcasts, afternoons in parks and coffee with sanity-saving friends. My rule of life is the school and nursery run, and my watching and waiting is done in doctors' and dentists' surgeries. I try to be a good partner, mother, daughter, sister, friend and Dean of Women Clergy. And in all of this I aspire to be a halfway decent priest and human being.

I am biorhythmically unable to be on my knees in prayer at 6 a.m. I can't manage a regular pattern of biblical study or theological reading. Extended periods of stillness and meditation are a thing of my distant past. Yet I think about God. A lot. When I write, when I speak, when I answer my children's questions and when I respond to strangers who want to know what my life as a priest is about. I think about what God is and means – in and through the world, other people and myself. I recognize signs of the presence of Love, and think I know when the miracle of creation is revealing itself to me.

I have had to find a different way of doing Sabbath, doing space and doing prayer, which gathers up and connects the myriad aspects of my life and makes some sense of them in the context of God. And it's a way that owes less to a 'rule of life' and much more to a passionate belief that God is in the air I breathe, the child I hold, the partner who holds me and the friends who encourage me to go to the spa once in a while. God touches me through the view from Hungerford Bridge, and the angel-fish in the aquarium. God connects with me through the gifted woman priest talking to me about her calling, and the wise, committed, hard-grafting men who have senior responsibility for the area of the London diocese in which I work. These are the people and events that delineate my life and give it meaning. For me Sabbath is meaning and definition and gift and grace.

If we can't find Sabbath of any kind, all the activity, relationships, impressions, loves and work become deadening rather than enlivening. We will capitulate to the culture of fatigue and the belief that we are all so endemically busy and incurably activity-driven that we can't grasp and experience any other way of being.

But Sabbath comes in various forms. So my argument is that we can do Sabbath in (at least) two ways – and that we must do it somehow. We can do it by quite literally setting apart time of a different quality. And we can do it by taking the activity and scramble of our day and approaching it with a Sabbath mentality – an approach that allows us to be more fully in the present moment.

Some of us need several approaches, in different measure. Some can live deeply and authentically by one or the other. So there is a truth in the idea that connection with God resides in the sorts of relationships and activities I've described above. There is a truth in the idea that we need to create space and silence in which to think consciously in the presence of God. And there's a truth in the idea that Sabbath requires us, sometimes, not even to think at all.

The Sabbath space we need is not created by clearing out what God has made and given. Rather it is the space within which the blessedness of God's giving and the sacredness of each day can be seen, honoured, embraced and loved.

10

Sitting loose to it all
Responding to frameworks and authorities

There have always been solitary Christians. Not everyone buys into the idea that in order to grow, faith needs to be nurtured in the context of a faith community. The theologian Paul Tillich took the debate even further with his cry,

> Forget all Christian doctrines; forget your own certainties and your own doubts, when you hear the call of Jesus . . . Nothing is demanded of you – no idea of God, and no good-ness in yourselves, not your being religious, not your being Christian, not your being wise and not your being moral.[1]

Tillich believed that when Jesus promised an easy yoke and a light burden[2] he was attempting to relieve people from the heavy load of religion – particularly the legalistic approach practised by some first-century Pharisees. He suggested that instead we are called simply to be open to the gift of God, who is the source and ground of our being, who freely offers love, and who longs that we might make an uncluttered and unfettered response.

But can we seriously explore God without any reference to an institutional religious framework? If we do not immerse ourselves in the regular retelling of the Christian story, how do we remember who we are and who God is? Without testing the boundaries of our belief against other people's thoughts and understanding, how do we know when we have grasped – or missed – the point? Is faith possible outside of this framework of checks and balances?

Of course it is possible. Lots of people sustain a lively belief in God without any involvement with the Church: those, for example, whose working life involves extensive travel and who are rarely in the same place long enough to establish a connection with a Christian community; people who are housebound and for some reason are unable to access regular contact with the local church; people who choose to be at home on Sundays with others who don't share their desire to worship; or people for whom close communities and rigid frameworks are a no-go area psychologically.

Among all of these people are those who genuinely believe, who are infused with the spirit of Christ, and whose lives reflect the characteristics of the God of justice and love and peace.

But are not most Christian believers irresistibly drawn to worship if it is there that we have a more intimate and felt experience of the living God? For ten years I worked in two different parishes, and the fundamental business of my working life was worship – the sort of worship that we easily recognize, the sort that takes place within four architecturally pleasing walls and requires a service sheet and the choice of appropriate hymns, words of Scripture, times of prayerful silence, and if we're lucky, the gift of sublime music.

Archbishop William Temple said, 'To worship is to quicken the conscience by the holiness of God, to feed the mind with the truth of God, to purge the imagination by the beauty of God, to open the heart to the love of God, to devote the will to the purpose of God.'[3] Many have experienced that quickening, feeding, purging and opening in the context of a praying community.

So yes, most believers are drawn to worship. But we don't do all our worship in a church and we don't do any of it in a vacuum. We do it with the material God has given us – each other, the created world, art, work, ideas, music, relationships. We take all that and more, and we try to work out where God is in it all, and to connect with God's activity and being. What quickens our conscience, feeds our mind, purges our imagination and opens our hearts is life itself.

Worship by this definition can provide a framework for our life, even outside of any 'belonging' to church. Because worship is about orientation. It's about what we turn towards and pay attention to.

It's about what we long for, what we love. If our understanding of what we are given to love is that each of these things is a grace and a gift of God to us, we worship through them all. Through people, music, sport, mountains – whatever turns us on, makes us tick, gives our life meaning. What matters is that we take seriously what we are orientated towards, what we are given to love – that we honour it, hold it in worth. Give it worth-ship and through it, perhaps, connect with God.

There have been three periods in my life when I have not worshipped regularly in a church. The first two were maternity leaves, lasting nine months each, during which time we were still living next door to the church in which I worked. Both times it simply felt that the spaciousness of not having to spend regular times in church was an unfamiliar luxury begging to be explored. That, coupled with the fact that taking a small baby to church – even if the church is next door – is a major expedition at the end of which the question 'Was it worth it?' is not always easily answered.

My more recent period of 'sparse' churchgoing followed on from leaving both my job and our home in Trafalgar Square. We moved house, settled the girls into school and a new nursery, and I felt my way into a very different set of commitments and responsibilities. While being wholly supportive of my vocation, my husband has no particular faith commitment and doesn't generally attend church. So this time round the gift was the sheer number of uninterrupted weekends to be spent as a family, being together and exploring a new part of town.

During all these sabbaticals from church it was glorious to enjoy Sabbath rest, rather than the complex Sunday timetable that had previously meant juggling church with family. And quite frankly, when the stuff of day-to-day life is ballet lessons and alphabet songs, lunch boxes, party invites and the latest *Dora the Explorer* DVD, church can be quite a cultural sea-change. If you do make it through the door you feel like an emissary from another world – a world just as real, but somehow in another reality from that of church!

Having set aside the discipline of church during my first maternity leave, I vividly remember asking myself whether I really wanted to take it up again. This soul-searching resulted in what a colleague termed my 're-entry sermon', when on my first

Sunday back I talked to the congregation about this time of sitting loose to the framework.

During that sitting loose I had questioned whether I needed the Church at all – and certainly whether or not it needed me. I had enjoyed ways of connecting with God in the world. I had weighed the merits and demerits of the institution, yet finally re-acknowledged its value. And I had discovered that in fact I am compelled by the truth of the gospel and the desire to preach it. I will probably always be drawn to doing so in the context of the gathering of believers, questioners and doubters that makes up each local incarnation of the Church of England.

So I have come back, three times, and chosen to engage with the framework of the Church once again. The experience of sitting loose for a time has not lessened my commitment, but has given me a different perspective. I now question how much we, as clergy, demand of lay people with terribly busy lives. I also question how much of what churches do has to be done by the church, or by that particular church as well as others. There's an endemic culture of taking everything on that sounds as though it might be important.

But I celebrate the Church's skill at holding in trust and retelling the stories of the Christian community, and encouraging people to find themselves in all of that. I recognize that the church at its best does hold us, nurture us, teach us, feed us and provide us with an extended human family. I understand that it can draw out of us what we believe, how we might live by it and how it might change us.

Yet I also know now that even for those of us who generally relate positively to this framework, there are times in our life when it might not work that well for us, when it is not what we need most. And at such times there are other ways in which we can grow in our faith.

Whether or not the Church's framework is one that we can live within, we do need landmarks in our lives if we are to drill deeper and not find ourselves faltering and disorientated. Those landmarks may be individuals whose wisdom and grace guide us through difficult times. They may be words – words of prose or poetry that inspire and direct us, assuring us of the road we must take. They may be the landmarks of the natural world, reminding us continually of God's power, fragility, intricacy, vulnerability, beauty and strength. They may be the landmarks of the built environment and human achievement, signposting us to the God who gives to humanity the most miraculous imagination and skills.

Alan Brownjohn's poem 'For a Journey' speaks of his wariness of travelling where landmarks are unknown and unnamed:

> So watch then, all the more carefully, for
> The point where the pattern ends . . .
> Who knows what could become of you where
> No one has understood the place with names?[4]

If you live in Basra, Jerusalem, the Gaza Strip or the Sudan, in a land where famine is endemic, or in a relatively young democracy where the process of political change is in its infancy, the landmarks – geographical, human and political – are constantly shifting. There is no pattern. A building that was there yesterday might not be there today. A child who was alive last night might not be this morning. A leader who was last week considered to have been democratically elected may not now seem quite so authentically the choice of the people.

And so life becomes an exercise in constant reorientation, with the need for extraordinary stamina and a very sure sense of self. In these circumstances people may increasingly seek inner landmarks that point to some power beyond themselves. It is this that enables many human beings to survive, and against all the odds survive creatively.

Alan Brownjohn's 'point where the pattern ends' is the point where the nervousness sets in. And this is a very common human experience. It seems that there's an umbilical connection between our ability to recognize and name the patterns and landmarks in the environment around us, and to take up our own authority and responsibility and live in that place creatively. And 'that place' might mean a literal, geographical environment. It might mean our own life or our own mind. Or it might mean the organization for which we work.

Clare Herbert is the Rector of Soho and was among the first women to be ordained priest in the Church of England. With insight, humour and, remarkably, no discernible bitterness, Clare has spoken and written about her experience – the experience of 20 years as a social worker exploring a priestly vocation that she could not actually live out as a priest and, since 1994, the experience of priesthood.

Clare talks lucidly about authority, and particularly the struggle to discern where it might come from. Speaking from the perspective of someone who for several decades was on the wrong side of a decision made by the authority of the Church, Clare speaks of finding an orientation that can grow only from a sense of your own God-given authority and self-worth. In her experience – and that of many women in the Church and other sectors – locating that authority means learning to rely less on the approval of the father figures of the Church, marvellous though some of them have been and are. We can only grow beyond that dependence on fatherly approval if we have the confidence to interpret the landmarks around us through our own, equally valid, perceptions.

This is not to suggest that we rely on our own perceptions to the exclusion of the authority vested, for good reason, in a larger framework and structure. We must, with wisdom, recognize the authorities around us and engage them in dialogue. Clare's image for living out a vocation in this new and strange landscape of a Church shaped by centuries of male hierarchy but now populated as well by a diversity of women, is the image of 'dancing in the desert'.

We live in and with landscapes and they shape our minds and lives: the landscape of the universe in all of its terrifying unknown vastness; the landscape of our world, changing, eroding, developing, being nurtured and destroyed and reclaimed and sustained; the landscape of each other's faces, endlessly traced, cherished and questioned; and our inner landscape, much of it unmapped, some of it all too familiar.

I am fascinated by John the Baptist, that original voice in the wilderness landscape. He seemed to have such a strong sense of inner authority and a confidence that he knew where God was in the landscape. When Jesus arrived at the River Jordan to be baptized[5] there was an instant realization that here was a greater authority – the one of which John had consistently spoken. He recognized its truth and authenticity with ease.

So I try, like John, to take up my own authority and speak of what I experience in the landscapes I inhabit. I hope to engage with the authority of the structures around me – and with those with whom I have differences – in a creative choreography that enables us all to dance a little closer to the Kingdom. In the difficult moments, when darkness falls and all the landmarks are obscured, I try to befriend that darkness and discover a new landscape within it that resonates with my own internal journey.

And I try ultimately not to be afraid of the unmapped road or the unnamed hill, but to walk it and climb it and to remember that every other religious leader has stood here, not sure whether they'll make it to the promised land. Where the patterns end, 'Who knows what will become of us?' I hold on to the hope that God does.

The Church as we experience it is a human institution, fallible and marvellous, frustrating and embracing. In moments when we feel let down, misunderstood or simply drained by the church, life outside its boundaries can point us back to God in a sudden shaft of understanding, grace, peace or inspiration. A friend who was thousands of miles away from her day job and from the church she both loves and wrestles with, meeting with people living in a dangerous place and connecting with their spirituality and faith, sent me a text. It simply said, 'I've remembered that I believe in God and how passionately Jesus challenged injustice.'

We sometimes need the grace of the world and its people to point us to the story the Church is telling. And we sometimes need the Church to tell that story in order that we may remember what a miracle the world is.

So we can sit loose to frameworks – the choice is ours – but equally they have much to offer us. We can accept and work with external authorities but we need a critically friendly, grown-up relationship with them. Landmarks can be helpful in enabling our own authority and orientation. Sometimes these will be outside of ourselves, and sometimes within.

Finally, when struggling to find our true orientation, it is at our peril that we ignore our instinctive longings. Rebecca Wells is author of the magnificently titled *Divine Secrets of the Ya-Ya Sisterhood* and its companion volume, *Little Altars Everywhere*. In *Little Altars* she follows one of the characters home for a family occasion. Siddalee Walker returns from her cosmopolitan life in Manhattan to Louisiana, in order to be godmother to her baby niece. Standing by the font, holding the child in her arms, she observes her family – which like most has its fair share of dysfunction. She tells us:

> My family stands in a circle around me. All the innocence, the old woundings. [And I feel it: the sweet pure longing of each of us, still intact.] This is what I come home to. I do not have to crawl across the desert on my knees. I do not have to swim through turbulent oceans to stop the drownings. I can hold the baby and not hurt her. I can hold them all and not hurt them. All I have to do is watch and pray, and love what I love.[6]

To be turned towards God is to watch and to pray, to hold and to love what we love, and in doing so, to go where that 'sweet pure longing' within takes us. And sometimes that will be easy, and a delight. But the realities of life include loss, pain, misunderstanding and disappointment, so sometimes it will be very, very hard.

Not all longings orientate us appropriately. They don't all turn us towards what is good and life-giving and creative. They don't all contribute to our wholeness. But some longings shape our lives for the better and help us to orientate ourselves. They are landmarks in themselves, pointers to where we should be going. They are part of the framework that keeps us in a creative place.

And of course in all of this the life of a believing community can be a great gift. As a priest I live in constant dialogue with the institution that has shaped the way I serve. I recognize that in some paradoxical sense the church is both superfluous and essential to my relationship with God and my growth in faith. Something similar might be said about other people's need of priests. In Alice Walker's novel *The Temple of My Familiar*, someone muses, 'As a minister, I am quite unnecessary to anyone else's salvation. Surely it is one of the universe's little jokes that I must be a minister in order to make them see this.'[7]

If we have the courage to grapple with the church in its failings and the ability to respond graciously to its eccentricities, in some times and places it can offer profound connections between ourselves, God and each other. If we want a grown-up relationship with the institution, then we have the inner authority to discover it. And together with the passion and the prose, the stories and the fragments of our existence, and the landmarks and longings, the framework of the church can be a sustaining and creative space in which to discover something of God.

11

Losing it entirely
Learning from our shadows

At junior school I bullied a girl in my class. Not just for one day. For a term or so, I think. And I persuaded everyone else to do it too. All but one girl, whose mother was a close friend of the bullied girl's mother. It stopped, not because of my guilty conscience, but because we were hauled into the headmistress's office for a good telling off. Twice, I seem to recall. So I guess I was pretty persistent.

We subsequently became friends, that gracious girl and I. But the memory of those actions still haunts me because the bullying was an expression of something real and something awful; something horrible in me that got out; something that I hope is now much diminished – I probably shouldn't delude myself that it's gone altogether.

We all live with our shadows, either more or less consciously. Psychologists would have us believe that the more consciously we can do it, the better. If we face our shadows and somehow deal with them – or at least learn to live with them – we can develop coping mechanisms, ways of living with the darkness and managing it as gently and positively as possible, ways of ensuring that the impact on other people is as little as it can be.

When our children were very small a rash of reality TV programmes about parenting found me frequently pointing the finger. As the on-screen tantrums escalated – and that was just the grown-ups – I found myself in accusatory mode: 'That's no way to relate to your children – no wonder they behave how they do – listen to that woman yell!'

Then I'd suddenly recall in vivid Technicolor some horribly unedifying incident with my own very young daughters, played out on the journey to nursery as we pushed through the throng of disapproving commuters, or in the privacy of our home and in the absence of cameras. Each incident recognizably at some point on the same spectrum of 'losing it, losing it badly and losing it spectacularly'. I realized that my indignation towards those parents on television was born of my own guilt, not anybody else's.

A wise grandmother once told me that our children bring out the worst in us. It made a fresh and honest change from all the talk about how they bring out our unselfish, unstinting, unswervingly caring selves. Being a carer for any highly dependent person – particularly in a personal rather than a professional capacity – forces us up against parts of ourselves we may not have known existed. We discover our extreme impatience, irrational anger and the desire to physically control someone when reasoning or respect don't seem to work. Our shadows and our dark side are very present here.

In the National Gallery there is a painting of a tug of war.[1] Not the sort where two teams of muscle-bound men pit their weight against each other. It's a tug of war between Christ's mother, Mary and a devout and elderly man called Simeon. Or between Christ's cosmic role as saviour of humanity and his own individual human life. Or between a faith community and a family. It depends which way you look at it.

The artist is known as the Master of the Life of the Virgin, and the episode in that life he depicts is Christ's presentation in the Temple, the occasion on which infant children were formally dedicated to God.[2] Mary is handing Jesus over to Simeon, who is about to proclaim his belief that in this child is the salvation of the world.

Although Mary's arms are fully outstretched she is still gripping the child as Simeon takes a firm hold from the other side to receive him. Christ is dead centre. Mary doesn't want to let Jesus go, and who can blame her? In the background of the painting is a picture of a story from the Hebrew Scriptures. It's Abraham, preparing to sacrifice his son Isaac.[3] So the artist reminds us of what was in Christ's future, and I find myself, as I look at the painting here and now, willing Mary not to let go of her child.

For Mary this was more than a tough call. Her path crossed with

God in a moment of collision that had cosmic consequences – and for her, bliss, followed by deep concern, then a tragic end. Utter, utter darkness. Of course the triumph of Easter was to come, but what that meant to her at the time we do not know and cannot guess. We can, however, imagine the desolation of her life as a result of his death.

By any way of looking at it Mary lost that tug of war. In spite of his best efforts, Jesus was not able to spare her any pain. The sword pierces her own heart also.[4] And so three decades later we find Jesus crucified, almost at the point of death, yet still desperately concerned for his mother. He sees his best-loved friend, John, standing near her: 'Woman behold thy son, behold thy mother.'[5] Mary, surely, is at best unconvinced. This is her darkest hour and there is no comfort or relief.

So the shadows and the darkness exist. We see them even at the heart of the gospel, and we know them in our own lives and the lives of others. This is not the nourishing and wondrous kind of darkness, but the harsh and punishing variety. In what ways does it manifest itself in our lives and the life of the world?

There are degrees of darkness of course. Some of the shadows are simply aspects of ourselves that are mildly unattractive. Some are a result of our mistakes. Some are cast by the bad decisions that are more deliberately and consciously made – we might call those our sin. Then there is the darkness of depression, which can descend inexorably for no apparent reason, refuse to shift for a very long time, and return without warning.

And there is the sort of shadowy darkness that is very much the flipside of an upside. We all know people who are incredibly gifted yet have one very big downside, which is the yin to the gift of their yang. (Or the yang to the gift of their yin – there are no intentional gender implications here!)

The 'mildly unattractive' stuff can be surprisingly hard to shift and takes myriad different forms. To name but a very few, it might be our habit of shutting others out of conversations when we're on a roll with our own opinions and stories; it might be the way we hold back from sharing an innovative idea at work simply because we are irritated by the person who's co-ordinating the project; it might be our inability to pass over another person's minor mistakes without comment; it might be our insistence that the fine details of domestic life are arranged according to our own taste and nobody else's.

We spend a lifetime offering such life-sapping habits up to God, praying that they will be dealt with and banished, only to discover that we've taken them back again. The only hope is that beyond this life we will be rid of them! Meanwhile we need to whittle away at the hold they have on us, hoping we'll make incremental improvements for the sake of those who also have to live with our foibles.

Travelling deeper into the shadows, beyond the mildly un-attractive stuff, we find the mistakes. Some mistakes cast shadows because, however innocently they were made, they have marred a relationship or a situation irretrievably. Others have the same effect but only because we cannot forgive ourselves our bad judgement, even if no long-term harm has been done. These are the shadows we need not live with, but it can take our most strong-minded efforts to shake them off.

Next comes the reality of sin. Most of us can identify at least some occasions when we've consciously gone ahead with saying or doing something we knew to be wrong. We know the conse-quences, the impact on others, the way sin debilitates us and our growth and diminishes our relationships with other people and with God.

Sometimes it helps if we review our day, our year or even our lives with the critical honesty that can bring us to a new under-standing of ourselves and the damage we can do. Looking back on our lives, there are apt reminders of how we fool ourselves into thinking that what we're doing is reasoned and appropriate, when it might well be self-evidently pretty awful.

Writing in the *Independent* in January 2005, the psychiatrist Professor Raj Persaud offered a psychodynamic perspective on how it is that British soldiers might be capable of enjoying the torture of Iraqi detainees.[6] His conclusion: an isolated group facing a perceived serious threat and insulated from independent judge-ments begins to engage in 'groupthink'. Eventually an unquestioning belief in their own moral superiority leads to the members of that group making wholly inappropriate responses to people outside its boundaries – all those who are perceived to be part of the threat. Everyone who is not a friend becomes an enemy.

This is a human psychological process, and the salutary truth is that not one of us is immune to it. It could have been us. What we are capable of when we believe that we have our backs to the wall is something we would do well to get a mental handle on. Acknowledging our possible responses might actually stop us from following through on the worst of them if the situation ever arose.

So there are shadows cast by our mildly unattractive characteristics, by our mistakes and by what we might call sin.

Then there is the darkness cast simply by what we might call, rather colloquially, the flipsides of our upsides. The most talented people sometimes get it the most badly wrong. History, literature, politics and drama are littered with such tragic heroes and heroines. Most have overreached themselves, or been seduced by the pressure into the relief of inappropriate relationships and behaviour, and lived to regret it.

Closer to home – and to our work and our social contexts – in the daily interplay of a complex web of relationships, all of which demand time and attention, we experience other people's downsides and we most probably know our own. We invest our time and care in building one another up and we feel shocked or let down when people's flipsides surface. Or when we fail to hide our own!

If we are to live deliberately and face things fully, perhaps we need to accept that this is an inevitable part of human relating. The occasions when we or others fall short of our best by a long way can be turned around if patience and an enduring love continue to undergird our relationships. What we can do for others is to try to embrace them as whole people, reflecting in our own attitude the spaciousness of God's grace, hoping that they will do the same for us – as the time will undoubtedly come when we need them to.

If we are to build healthy relationships and live a fertile life, it is essential to find a level of self-understanding that enables us to mitigate the harm our flipsides do to others. We need to be as rigorously honest with ourselves as we dare.

Finally there is a particularly life-sapping experience of the shadows Winston Churchill famously called 'black dog'. Statistics suggest that 'seven to 12 per cent of men suffer from diagnosable depression, and 20 to 25 per cent of women'.[7] I was stopped on the street recently by a charity fundraiser who asked, 'Do you know anyone suffering from depression?' 'Probably,' I replied, and the fundraiser caught the irony in my tone and smiled ruefully. Priests – spending time as they do with those who need desperately to talk to someone who will keep their counsel – are well placed to know just exactly how pervasive depression is in contemporary Western society. In fact most people, priests or not, know others whose lives are blighted by the condition.

When I was a child, a woman – it was usually a woman – suffering from anxiety or depression was said to be 'bad with her nerves'. Nowadays we are more willing to tell it as it is. Yet in spite of society's increased understanding that depression exists, is common and is horribly real, sufferers still come across a lack of understanding in many people. It's part of the darkness of the experience.

What do we do if we are unfortunate enough for that shadow to descend on us? God can work through the diagnosis of a good GP, the professional assistance of counsellors and therapists of all kinds, and the offer of appropriate medication. For those suffering from 'black dog', anti-depressants can quite literally be a lifeline. They may protect people from the permanent damage that can be sustained when fighting an unwinnable fight.

But people who use this medication will tell us that, while essential to making life liveable, it doesn't bring back the warmth and light of 'life without depression'. In fact it often takes the edge off everything, effectively removing light and shade, levelling everything out so that there are no lows, but no highs either.

Many people who suffer in this way – whether or not they access any of these resources – speak of having to wait out the time until the shadows lift and life begins, slowly, to return to some semblance of normality, to a rhythm of highs and lows and in-betweens that is acceptable and balanced. Until this happens, all they can do is trust that God holds them in love. That is, if they can make the mental leap of thinking about God in positive terms, or at all.

The need to maintain our own sense of balance, not to allow the universe to wrong-foot us, is a strong instinct. Our ability to make bad decisions, to be spectacularly wrong when we're certain we're right, the way the whole thing can come crashing in overnight, the fragility of our health, of relationships, of our world – all of these things can plunge us into the shadows.

So the image of a tug of war remains with me. Mary's fight. It speaks to me of the reality of a shadow side in the created order. It exists. And we wrestle with it, trying all the while to maintain the balance and coherence of our lives. We try to thrust away the demons, or determinedly pull towards us all that is life-giving. This struggle is variously a tug of war or a wrestling match or just a fist fight. The image that fits best will depend on the sorts of shadows we're struggling with. But all of these processes take energy and courage and the determination to live through the experience.

We cannot, for the most part, untangle how much of this is our own careless doing, as individuals and as a collective human race – and how much is a result of the tragic possibilities inherent in the nature of a creation that is the work of an artist and lover. We tell ourselves that God will, with extravagant, love-ridden gestures, work the tragedies into a deeper beauty across the canvas. But that is no comfort here and now, living in the darkness. For me, Mary's dark story is iconic – pointing to the truth and pain of this process – because it is the story of tragedy pointing to eventual triumph, but is experienced by her as an individual simply as the darkest nightmare.

'And they crucified him.'[8] Mary watches her son, rent on the cross, and remembers with irony his words to the crowd of women by the roadside on the way to the crucifixion site. 'Daughters of Jerusalem, weep not for me. Weep for yourselves and for your children.'[9] But he *is* her child. And this is where it is to end. How is it that here she is, among the faceless wailing multitude, weeping for him?

How angry Mary must have been with God. How far she must have felt from any trace of his love. How exiled in her grief by the one who had entrusted her with bearing and parenting the Word made flesh – and then somehow allowed all of this to be part of what she must hold and live with in trust.

We are angry for her, as we are angry with God for creating a world in which there is the possibility of having to live with such depths of despair. The universe has a shadow side. How well we human beings know this. The effect of HIV and AIDS, the impact of natural disaster, terminal illness, the horrors perpetrated on others by those whose inner darkness eventually explodes and deposits its fall-out.

All of these experiences are hard and shadowy and excruciatingly painful – and so very, very real. The sheer weight of them can push individuals, communities, even nations below the reach of the light.

Yet in faith we hold on to the hope that in some way God presides over this universe by which we are all hurt as well as healed, shaken as well as held. That God is to be encountered in the darkness and in those who share that darkness with us.

In the shadows – of whatever sort – people turn to many God-given gifts to alleviate their sorrow. We are comforted by music, art, friendship, humour, rare sunlight, sex and the telling of stories. 'In the dark times/Will there also be singing?' asked Bertolt Brecht, and answered himself: 'Yes, there will also be singing/About the dark times.'[10]

12

'I want to stay here'
Living with our mortality

—◆—

During one Lent season when she was three years old, Hannah and I did death in a big way. It was painful for both of us. We started with *The Lion King* and the tragic demise of Simba's father, who was trampled by wildebeests during an attempt to rescue his young son – effectively murdered by his jealous brother who had plotted the whole thing. The story led to Hannah's poignant and repeated question, 'Mummy, why has Simba's Daddy gone to heaven if Simba can't follow him there?'

We then took out a library book about a very, very, very old dog called Daisy. Daisy goes to sleep one night and wakes up in heaven, where she is reunited with all her canine friends. But Daisy continues to worry about Arthur, the little boy she has left behind, so she keeps an eye on him and sends him dreams. In this way she lets him know that it is beautiful in heaven, she is happy, and that it's okay by her if he gets a new dog. Which Arthur, once he's worked through the five stages of bereavement, does.[1]

So three-year-old Hannah learnt that 'in the end' – a phrase she rather caught onto – 'in the end we'll all go to heaven'. She was anxious about arriving there to find that Mummy and Daddy had been delayed, because then she'd be lonely. So there was a difficult dynamic being negotiated. We needed to reassure her that in the natural course of things Mummy and Daddy ought to get there first, without tipping her off too clearly as to what that means in the here and now.

Through a mixture of child-like directness and adult existential angst, we got somewhere. Heaven at least became common parlance in our household. So much so that on a particularly balmy morning in a warm, sunny, hedge-enclosed area of Embankment

Gardens, Hannah looked at the blue sky, the vibrant spring foliage and the sun playing on the paving and declared 'We are in heaven. I want to stay here.'

Later that same year my father died. I have, in my decade as a priest, spent many hours with those who are grieving the loss of loved ones. I have tried to be there as a support, as a resource, as someone who in a particular role and by their own faith represents the hope of the reality of resurrection – of something beyond what we know here and now.

Over the years people have told me that it has been steadying to have someone there in that role. I've frequently been thanked for 'doing a good funeral' and been told, sincerely I think, that it has helped. I have meant what I've said in offering that hope and that resurrection faith. And I still do. But none of that prepared me for the reality of losing someone close to me, and what death does to those left behind. The tangible absence. The terror of the question 'Where is he?', and the greater terror of 'Is he anywhere at all?'

Douglas Board, in his collection of thoughts and prayers *The Naked Year*, speaks about the quiet decimation bereavement brings.

Almighty God
You have spun our lives like gossamer between the stars
Each strand held in your hands.
You show us that you love us
And tell us death is not the end.

But this morning
The mirror looked at my cracked face
And the cold sink winced under my raging hands
Until the plughole confessed
That my life had been poured away yesterday.

So I shan't do astral gossamer today, if that's all right with
    you.[2]

In a clergy staff meeting very early in my time at St Martin-in-the-Fields, someone commented 'Of course, we do Good Friday at St Martin's much better than we do Easter. Because we do Good

Friday all of the time.' St Martin's is a church that lives with reality, lives with the mess of our lives and our world, lives with human
experience as it is for some people much of the time and for most
of us some of the time – painful, hard, uncompromising.

So in that place we sat with the marginalized and the depressed
as they wandered in during the week and found a space where they
would be taken seriously. We opened our doors to people whose
homes were no longer a place where they could feasibly live. We
did Good Friday all of the time.

But what did we offer of Easter? Rubem Alves, the Brazilian
theologian, psychoanalyst and philosopher, has said, 'Hope is
hearing the melody of the future. Faith is to dance to it.'[3] My final
Easter at St Martin's, the first after my father's death, found me
unable to tango and able to say only this:

I'm not quite dancing this Easter morning, and there will be
many of you who aren't either. I'm not sufficiently certain
of the melody of what's beyond this life to abandon myself
to it. And that's simply because it's the first Easter since my
father fell to his death from a mountain in the Lake District,
and therefore the first on which I've been unable to picture
where someone I deeply love actually is. I'm by no means
alone in this.

Of course even without the resurrection the gospel story
is captivating – from its declaration that 'In the beginning was the Word' right up to Calvary. It teaches us about
God manifest in creation, about fullness of life in all of its
aspects, about the wonder of human community and the
fertile possibilities when life is lived at peace with one
another and with God. All of that holds without Easter.

But in the end, when push comes to shove, if on this Easter
Day heaven is not – as our early morning liturgy told us –
wedded to earth, fused by love and glory, there is something
singularly lacking in the story's end.

I know the ending I want – I want Isaiah's mountain-top
feast, the rich food, the well-aged wines strained clear. I want
to know in my body that death has been swallowed up for
ever, and that the God whom I have worshipped all of my
life will wipe the tears from the eyes of all who mourn. I want

to know, with the conviction of Peter, that God raised Jesus on the third day. I want to see the mortician's linen wrappings thrown to the side because he has no more need of them. And I want that to be true of everyone we have all known and loved and held and belonged to, whom we can no longer talk with or touch.[4]

David Monteith, one of the first friends I made in London, had sent me a poem that Holy Week about Michelangelo's *Rondanini Pietà*. The sculpture is of Mary the mother of Christ supporting the body of her dead son from behind in a kind of slumped standing position – knees buckling as he, a dead weight, blends with her and she becomes an exquisite combination of fragility and strength.

It's an unfinished piece, and as I researched its story on the internet one website told me: 'The non-finished work appears to embody the value of a fragmented idea, which the author was not able (or did not want) to express unless by broken phrases . . .'[5]

There are things that only broken phrases will express. In that case, the anguish of Mary holding her son in death. In our case, the hope of resurrection. How can we say or describe it? Words slip through our fingers like sand.

The poem that related to the sculpture is by David Scott. Of the entwined figures it says that the two are somehow carrying one another. And Scott focuses on the bent knees of the figure of Christ, telling us that although they are broken they are ready to spring, and that the entire world – which he now imagines Jesus to be carrying – is waiting for that moment, 'crying, "now!"'[6]

We are on his back, crying now. We desperately need to know that he can do it, that it's for real, that whatever the death is that we experience in the midst of our life – whether it is lack of something, loss of someone, brokenness of spirit, unbearable fragility of heart – and because of the death we will all come to in the end, our need is to know that Christ can transform it and be raised – because if he can, perhaps so can we.

Perhaps St Martin's is better at doing Good Friday than Easter, but then Easter is so much harder to do. We don't know how to describe the offer, the reality of something that is so hard to understand and to touch, something in which we invest such hope. As a friend said to me that particular Easter Day, our faith may be secure, but on these things it might not be certain.

Yet I hold to the belief that one day, in spite of our broken knees, we will dance to the music of the resurrection.

Many will recognize from their own experience the twin truths of my security and my uncertainty – and my longing to know that eternity is a time and a place that will ultimately enfold us all in the fullness of its Sabbath. I have a picture of God as creator, redeemer, friend, fell-walker, flamenco-dancer, strengthener of broken bones and inventor of Easter. I place my hope in the sacrificial, risk-taking spring of those shattered knees. And I try to live by the tentative tenacity of that hope.

There's a painting by Titian that always makes me angry, and fills me with hope. It's of Mary Magdalene at the tomb with the risen Christ, and it's called *Noli me tangere*. Do not touch me. Hence my anger at the fact that he asked Mary not to do what she most needed. No amount of reassurance that the Greek, accurately translated, actually means 'Do not cling' rather than do not touch, takes that anger away. Yet the painting also evokes hope, wonder, miracle and tremendous possibility. I love it and I hate it, at one and the same time.

We bring all of that cocktail with us each Easter Day, and every day that death brushes by us with its certain and sure wings. We want to touch the miracle of the resurrection – really touch it – and we know that we can't. We believe that the reality God offers is so much more than that which we can imagine, yet we wish it might be translated into something that is tangible in our own terms. What I love about the Titian painting I also find most painful. Its uncompromising depiction of the hope and the harshness of human experience – both of which are real and true. A window we cannot climb through onto an eternity we can glimpse yet not grasp.

Like Mary, what we really need is the concrete proof of holding and being held. But our faith is in what we cannot touch. Like Mary, from this complex place within ourselves we proclaim with the fragile strength of all our being: 'I have seen the Lord.'[7]

In all of this, of course, we are not only fearful of losing loved ones. We live with the knowledge of our own mortality. I'm afraid I'm not (yet) with St Paul when he confidently declares 'to me, living is Christ and dying is gain.'[8] There's still so much that I love, of and in this world. Detachment is not even a remote option.

Yet to refuse to contemplate the finite nature of our life as we know it is surely the action of a particularly stubborn ostrich. The certainty of death and taxes demands that if we are to live honestly, deliberately and in the spirit of looking reality levelly in the face, we have to have some hold on this issue, some way of addressing it in the context of our daily lives, without being morbid or allowing the reality of death to diminish the fullness of our experience here and now, but also without the impotence and dishonesty of avoiding what is undeniably real.

We have a painting in our flat that some people love and others are deeply puzzled by. The bottom part of the canvas is painted in yellows, ochres and browns, climbing steeply and finishing in an abrupt and uneven way roughly halfway up the canvas. The top section, the remaining half, is painted in several shades of off-white. So the overall impression is perhaps of a cliff face against a starkly blank sky. Many of our friends see it as a half-finished picture of something they can't identify – and that's when they are being polite.

The painting, by Gill Hickman, is called *Where I Am and Where I'd Love to Be*. I love it for its ambiguity. Are these two different places, and if so does the artist want to be part of that rich and redolent 'earth', or the white space beyond? Or is she saying that they are two separate places, one where she is and one where she'd like to be? Or, a third possibility, is she in some sense in both places and happy with both?

It strikes me that the painting offers an image of our struggle with what we know and what we don't know; with the earth and heaven that we believe to be inextricably part of the same universe and reality, yet which we also experience as 'differently' real and undeniably apart; with the knowledge of life as it is – in all its colours – coupled with our curiosity about what might yet be to come; with our desire to stay with the familiar, even in difficult times, just because it's what we know and because the 'not knowing' of the beyond can be terrifying, coupled with our hope that there might be something else that takes up and completes our essential incompleteness.

Following the image through, there's a sense in which our life is delineated by that point on the canvas where the ochres, yellows and browns end and the whites begin. The fact of something beyond what we know – or at least our faith in something beyond – somehow focuses and holds the here and now in a helpful way. This is hard to articulate. Zadie Smith makes a helpful attempt in her novel *On Beauty*. Kiki Belsey, mother of three, wife of a husband who has recently slept with an unknown woman, tired and weary of trying to keep the family on track, is in a park one lovely evening. Together with her family she's listening to an outdoor orchestral performance. It prompts in her wandering mind the following thoughts.

> Mozart's Requiem begins with you walking towards a huge pit. The pit is on the other side of a precipice, which you cannot see over until you are right at its edge. Your death is awaiting you in that pit. You don't know what it looks like or sounds like or smells like. You don't know whether it will be good or bad. You just walk towards it. Your will is a clarinet and your footsteps are attended by all the violins. The closer you get to the pit, the more you begin to have the sense that what awaits you there will be terrifying. Yet you experience this terror as a kind of blessing, a gift. Your long walk would have had no meaning were it not for this pit at the end of it.[9]

Our lives are framed by birth and death, and without one or other of those things they would not be coherent. This is the way things are. This is the inescapable reality of our existence. Once birth has happened death is not an optional extra, it's an odds-on certainty. We need to live with that. We need to allow it to influence our decision-making.

Does that mean living cautiously in an attempt to ensure that death is put off until the last possible moment? Some do take this approach, and quite understandably. Others react by living for the here and now, grasping opportunities when they come, initiating new ventures when they see their possibility even faintly on the horizon. For most of us there's probably a conversation to be had between the two approaches, and the attempt to live a full and meaningful life is about balancing the risk of shortening it with the risk of not really living it at all.

In the cold weary light of January, some weeks after my father's death, Hannah and I were again in Embankment Gardens. We walked through the sheltered, hedge-enclosed area on our way back from visiting the fishpond, and through the part of the garden that Hannah had associated with heaven on that kinder day the previous spring. It was the first time we'd been there since my father died. Hannah, with a sudden joyful quickening, said 'It's Heaven. Where's Grandad?'

With a sinking feeling that this was to be the first serious hurdle in the development of her faith, I took a deep breath and said 'This is *pretend* heaven, Hannah – Grandad's in the real heaven, isn't he, so he won't be here.' She was back at me like lightning and with the unfailing logic and conviction of a four year old: 'But *pretend* Grandad's here, isn't he?'

The boundaries between where we are and where we will be one day are difficult for us to fathom and more difficult for us to live with. But this is the reality of it. Our healthy survival and growth in this world, and the deepening of our relationship with the God who made it this way, depend on that most delicate of juggling acts – the ability to love deeply where we are and to be ready to spring at the moment when, for us, heaven cries 'now'.

13

Six degrees of separation
The courage to connect

The social psychologist Stanley Milgram believed that everybody in the world can be linked to everybody else in six stages. In other words, that there are only six degrees of separation between all of us. If I know you and you know someone else and we follow that process through six stages, we will find that the web of connection is complete – everyone is linked to everybody else.

I'm not a mathematician so I won't try to prove the hypothesis, but some people have attempted it. Although the number of required links has differed from study to study, it has consistently been found to be small. If Milgram was right, there are phenomenal implications for the wellbeing of humanity. So much hangs on our ability to make friends rather than enemies. How finely balanced is the world's equilibrium.

'Only connect! That was the whole of her sermon. Only connect the prose and the passion, and both will be exalted, and human love will be seen at its height. Live in fragments no longer.'[1]

Margaret Schlegel, in E. M. Forster's novel *Howards End*, has woken up to the fact that her fiancé's fundamental problem is his complete lack of awareness. He is ignorant of what lies within and beyond him and between other people, and how all of that relates. He can't connect – with himself, with others or with the world.

Sometimes I feel as though 'only connect' is the whole of my sermon too. Being a priest is about making connections, connections between God and the world, Jesus and God, the world and ourselves, ourselves and God and between each other. To connect is to live with some sense of entirety and wholeness. To discover our place in the world, and our meaning, is to open ourselves to fullness, and to healing.

Life offers numerous 'connecting agents'. For some of us poetry is an effective one. It connects what Margaret Schlegel calls 'the prose and the passion'. It frees us to interpret more wholly and experience more deeply the things that we can't necessarily explain in prose. And the prose of our lives – the narrative, the story, the events – is in turn enlivened and more fully understood because of the poetry.

Images, too, can be connectors. They point us towards things beyond words – things that are true and that the image helps us to know. Giles Fraser, vicar, writer and broadcaster, has written:

> For as long as I can remember, I have loved London as if she were a friend. I love her colour, her energy, her size, her age; this morning it was her beauty. The Thames is the life that flows through her body – always the same, always new. It sustains the city; it is ever present; I will never know its depths. For me, the Thames is liquid theology.[2]

'Liquid theology' was an image that I took into the next day, and the next. It was an invitation, as I went about my life as part of the city's pulsing, to make connections between God and the environment around me and to let those connections flow.

If poetry and images connect us with what is within and outside us, then so does memory. The suffering of people with Alzheimer's disease is a graphic illustration of what happens when we are disconnected from our memories. With intermittent memory people struggle to identify strands of meaning, to make sense of themselves, to connect with their past, and therefore their present, and with who they are. The painful task of holding them together is left to others, who do it partly by trying to reconnect them with an understanding of themselves and therefore who they are and what they 'mean'.

In better times memories can help us to discern the things that are for growth in our lives and the things that can damage us. When memories are faced with wisdom and honesty, they can point us to what is good. They can point us to God, who nurtures us onwards into a more creative future.

In Helen Simpson's short story, 'Constitutional', a woman tries to make sense of the death of a friend by exploring an idea from the world of neuroscience. It's about how the act of remembering changes the map of our brain. Apparently when we remember, we're not just taking a video off a mental shelf and watching it, we're chasing an original memory and reconstructing it. Every time we do it we strengthen that neural pathway.

So the narrator says of her late friend Stella,

> If it is true that each established memory makes a track, a starry synaptic trail in the brain, and that every time we return to . . . that particular constellation of memory, we strengthen it, then so is the following. Stella's billion lucent constellations may have been extinguished at her death, but she herself has become part of my own brain galaxy, and part of the nebulous clusters of all her myriad friends. Every time I remember Stella, I'll be etching her deeper into myself . . .[3]

A connection between two friends is reinforced, even physically embedded. The dead woman remains connected to the world. And as we remember those we grieve for, they are made real in us, and continue to be intertwined with the fabric of the world. They are here because everything they touched has their imprint and is imbued with their influence, and because we remember them and we are still here. To affirm that is in some sense to keep them alive, to ensure that the connection is still real.

The act of remembering – of connecting – lies at the very heart of the Christian story. 'Do this in remembrance of me' says Jesus just before his death. The events that followed suggest that he didn't just mean that his friends should replay a mental video. He was asking them to make his presence real in their own time and space. So as we remember him, Jesus is made real in us – that is one way in which he is part of the present.

But there is another sense in which Jesus' life and his very self connected people – with one another and with God: through healing. Whether it is physical, emotional or psychological, healing demands an openness to what human beings can do for one another and what God can do if we are willing to risk the subversive power of the Creator's grace.

Connection is so much the basic stuff of life that it's almost the air we breathe. Yet we don't always welcome, encourage or explore connections fully. It takes courage to take hold of some strands of connection – with difficult memories, with people we find hard work or threatening, with questions about ourselves and the world that we can't answer and with the God whom we often feel we don't know or understand.

In Matthew's Gospel we meet a woman who was not afraid of difficult encounters, in spite of the shame that she carried with her. 'Then suddenly a woman who had been suffering from haemorrhages for twelve years came up behind him and touched the fringe of his cloak.'[4]

There is something about the image of a haemorrhage that shocks and frightens us. Perhaps it's because it's a graphic picture of life literally draining away – and the desperate need to hold on to it. Even if it isn't potentially fatal, a severe loss of blood is debilitating. Anyone who has ever suffered from anaemia as a result of such a loss will say that until the condition is corrected or corrects itself, life is lived with a diminished capacity – the ability to take only shallow breaths, the disproportionate effort required to do anything at all.

The woman who touched the fringe of Jesus' cloak had lived this way for 12 years. Yet she can still believe that all she needs to do is touch him and she will be healed. Her faith is astounding. It meets with Jesus' power and the healing takes place. He channels her faith towards the possibility of healing, not in a crude 'If you believe, it will happen; if you don't, it won't' sort of way, but with the more oblique 'Your faith has made you well'.

We don't always give ourselves the opportunity to be made well or made whole. There are situations in our lives where the blood is running out. Unresolved conflicts within ourselves; relationships that went wrong – and although retrievable that we have continued to neglect; desires it might be possible to fulfil but that it has been easier to suppress.

Connecting is sometimes tougher than avoidance, more of a challenge. It's easier to live in a bubble, if we have the choice, especially when connecting is with difficult and different people.

But if the 'other' in others is also the other in ourselves and in God, we need the courage to connect if we are to be fully what we are meant to be. If the many different selves we actually are all reflect different truths, we need to trace the connections between them in order to grow more fully into our whole self.

Yet sometimes we continue to allow the lifeblood to run out. We do not reach out or reach in for potential sources of healing, perhaps because it feels risky or demands the willingness to be vulnerable to another or to ourself, perhaps because our coping mechanisms have become a way of life and without them we would have to rethink who we are. What we aren't facing is the probability that slowly, in some area of life, we are dying unnecessarily. Our God-given potential is gradually being haemorrhaged away. Even if the process is so slow that it is not life-threatening, it is still life-diminishing. Darkness and shadows threaten.

Along with many other people, for some time now the economist Jeffrey Sachs has been reminding us that we can and must connect, globally. Our lives depend on it and so does the life of our planet. Ongoing conflicts across the globe are a continued reminder of the destruction that follows in the wake of the disconnection of peoples, in the wake of the inappropriate use of connections (such as unhelpfully handled interventions in the lives of other states), in the wake of the cowardly refusal to intervene even in the face, for example, of mass genocide. The lifeblood runs out if we don't connect at the right time with the right situations.

So poetry, images and memory are potential connectors, if we're looking to them for that purpose. Christ connects us with a source of healing that is ours to embrace if we have the courage – and reminds us that the lifeblood runs out in certain situations if we don't engage, as it will, if we don't act well and swiftly enough, for the created world, which is a powerful source of connection with God and with the deeper rhythms of our own lives, if we allow it to be.

The spring equinox has given me pause for thought in recent years. I've begun to realize that the rhythms of my life and energy are more tied into the changing seasons than I previously thought – or perhaps than they previously were. This sense of connection refers me back to my childhood, a time of intense awareness of the year's changes, terms, seasons and festivals.

My renewed consciousness of that is probably partly because the seasons are changing in themselves, with early springs, warmer than average summers and less rainfall. So I notice them more.

It may also be about watching our daughters respond to them. And it may – as I approach the end of my fourth decade – be about age, some growing sense of my own 'waxing and waning' alongside the annual cycle of birth, death and renewal.

I'm not alone. More than one person of roughly my age has told me that the most recent spring equinox effected an almost miraculous rush of new energy and alertness – not quite the rising of sap but a pretty similar experience! For me this followed a definite period of wanting to hibernate – a reluctance to leave the warmth of the duvet and a preference for days spent at home with the girls playing games, making things and watching DVDs, rather than gritting my teeth and making a dash for the wind-swept reaches of Regent's Park.

The created world is one of the sources of connection that influences our pace. If we can allow it to slow us down we may stop and notice more, find more Sabbath moments and perceive God in the littlest of things. Its vibrancy can encourage in us new life, new ideas, new energy.

Finally, one of the greatest sources in our lives of engagement with ourselves and God is the relationship we have to other people. C. S. Lewis once commented: 'In each of my friends there is something that only some other friend can fully bring out.'[5] Other people play a fundamental part in enabling us to be fully who we are.

In parts of Africa this truth is encapsulated and given flesh in the phenomenon of ubuntu. Ubuntu is all about connections. People understand and translate the word in various subtly different ways, but essentially it's about relationships and the idea that we are formed by our connections with others. Our very self is shaped and fulfilled by others and our connections with them.

So I am what I am because you are what you are. I become human through my relationships with the rest of humanity. Ubuntu is what causes us to connect with strangers in need and to recognize our utter dependency on other people – both practically and in terms of understanding ourselves.

Milgram's theory of six degrees of separation has tremendous power if we can only live by the ubuntu conviction that I am what I am because I am connected with you. This is an unimaginably huge challenge, but do we have any choice but to take it on?

The fabric of our existence is the touch, the scent, the taste, the sight, the loveliness and the unloveliness of ourselves and other people. This is the context in which we live out the fullness of our humanity and become all that God would have us be, in the same way that God can only be fully God when we are authentically ourselves.

And this intricately woven fabric of human interdependence is how it is meant to be. In spite of some of the hard things that Jesus said about human relating and the need, sometimes, for a greater degree of detachment, the fact is that he went to his own death out of a passionate commitment to the women and men among whom he had lived his life, and those who had gone before and those who were still to come. They were not an abstract concept but a human community, with whom he had walked, slept, eaten, laughed, cried and sweated blood.

A couple of years ago I found myself in a large gathering of clergy praying and singing together. We sang a song I'd sung countless times before, and with complete conviction, in another spiritual incarnation called the university Christian Union. 'As the deer pants for the water so my soul longs after you', we began sweetly. But that was as far as I could get. I could not sing 'you alone are my heart's desire . . . I want you more than any other' *because it isn't true.*

I love God, but my love for certain other people and theirs for me is much more immediate, and insistent. There are some I might possibly die for – but I can't say, even with that dubious level of conviction, that I would die for God. And incidentally, Psalm 42 on which the song is supposedly based speaks only of a longing for God, not of love for God set over and against love for each other.

The love of human beings – between men and women, between men, between women, between friends, colleagues, children and parents – is the fullest image available to us of the love of God. We know this. We are made in God's image and this is the primary evidence of it.

Rowan Williams writes, 'Only the body saves the soul . . . left to itself the inner life is not capable of transforming itself. It needs the gifts that only the external life can deliver: the actual events of God's action in history, heard by physical ears . . . and the actual, wonderful, disagreeable, impossible, unpredictable human beings we encounter daily . . . Only in this setting do we become holy.'[6]

To be holy is to be working towards wholeness and entirety, in such a way that our ordinariness is seen to be the miracle that it is, whole and entire in such a way that the connection between all life becomes more evident and more potent in our own lives.

I'm left wondering whether this book has any hint of wholeness or entirety to it. Or is it simply a series of random statements, stories and thoughts? Is there some sort of coherent whole or just an array of unrelated fragments?

Whatever the answer to that question, I end with the conviction that we need to connect. We need to connect with the reality of our doubts; with the potential of risk; with all the people that we are; with 'the other' in ourselves and others and God; with our real desires; with our hankering after perfection and our need for entirety.

We must connect with our fertility in all its forms; with the small things in our day in which God's life is encapsulated; with our need for Sabbath and a Sabbath way of living; with the internal and external authorities that enable us to set our compass; with our darkness and our shadows; and with the mortality of those we love, the inevitability of our death and all our questions about what comes next.

> Only if we connect are we living life deliberately.
> Only if we connect can we become fully ourselves.
> Only if we connect can the creation be healed entirely.
> And only if we connect can God be fully God.

Conclusion

For now we see in a mirror, dimly – but then we will see face to face. Now I know only in part; then I will know fully, even as I have been fully known.

1 Corinthians 13.12

So we have seen something of what it might mean to live deliberately. To face life full on without attempting to protect ourselves from its complex and nuanced realities. We have decided to do this because we believe that it's the best way to grow, and we suspect that otherwise we will die realizing that we have not actually lived.

Our trajectory traces ever widening circles: through the reality of doubt and risk; via the challenge of our several selves and everything that difference and envy can teach us; from perfectionism to entirety; by way of a redefined fertility, the magic of the small, and a need for Sabbath; through longings and via landmarks, with our accompanying shadows and in full knowledge of our mortality and that of those we love.

Finally we have concluded that we must 'only connect'. It is vital not to mistake the *only* for that which implies little effort. Rather it is the only that means 'this is all that matters – nothing more'.

We seek to connect with the other. The other in people, in God, and most certainly in ourselves. Such connections will transform us so that we are more wonderfully alive. And so that God is more gloriously present in the world.

'Then we shall see face to face' writes St Paul. A friend tells me that he loves to take issue with Paul's use of the word *then*. Because in fact *then* is – at least partially – *now*. Eternal life does not just come afterwards. We begin the process of seeing and experiencing it more fully at whatever point we are on the spiral – not waiting until it carries us to a more rarefied place. Even in our partially sighted phase we begin to grasp eternity, because as well as being *there* it is very much *here*.

In our moments of seeing more entirely, the biggest challenge is that of perceiving *ourselves* as we are and being able to bear that knowledge in such a way that we are changed and made more fully alive, that here in the world we might reflect more completely the grace, fertility and love of God – our entire and deliberate Creator.

Notes

Introduction

1 Henry David Thoreau, *Walden* (Harmondsworth, Penguin, 1983), p. 135.
2 Irenaeus, *Against Heresies*, vol. 4 (Kila, MT, Kessinger, 2004), ch. 20.

1 In the absence of a Green Room

1 Lauris Edmond, 'Applied Astronomy', in *New and Selected Poems* (Newcastle upon Tyne, Bloodaxe Books, 1992), p. 74. Reproduced by permission of the Literary Estate of Lauris Edmond.
2 Edmond, 'Applied Astronomy', p. 74. Reproduced by permission of the Literary Estate of Lauris Edmond.
3 Isaiah 9.2.
4 Isaiah 45.3.
5 J. R. R. Tolkien, *The Lord of the Rings, Part Three: The Return of the King* (London, George Allen and Unwin, 1955), p. 302.
6 *All Things Considered*, broadcast on BBC Radio Wales, 19 March 2006.
7 Theodore Roethke, 'The Waking', in *Staying Alive* (Tarset, Bloodaxe Books, 2002), p. 106. 'The Waking', copyright © 1953 by Theodore Roethke, from COLLECTED POEMS OF THEODORE ROETHKE by Theodore Roethke. Used by permission of Doubleday, a division of Random House, Inc. Theodore Roethke, 'The Waking', in *Collected Poems* (Faber and Faber, 1968). Used by permission.

2 Managing without God

1 Dietrich Bonhoeffer, *Letters and Papers from Prison*, ed. Eberhard Bethge, trans. Reginald Fuller and others, rev. edn (New York, Macmillan, 1967), p. 188.
2 Luke 21.25–26.
3 Paul Seabright, *The Company of Strangers* (Princeton, NJ, Princeton University Press, 2005), p. 15.
4 Mark 15.31.
5 Denise Levertov, 'Immersion', in *This Great Unknowing: Last Poems* (Tarset, Bloodaxe Books, 2001), p. 52. By Denise Levertov, from THIS GREAT UNKNOWING: LAST POEMS, copyright © 1999 by The Denise Levertov Literary Trust, Paul A. Lacey and Valerie Trueblood

Rapport, Co-Trustees. Reprinted by permission of New Directions Publishing Corp.

6 Nora Gallagher, *Things Seen and Unseen: A Year Lived in Faith* (New York, Vintage Books, 1994), p. 4.

7 Interview with Béla Tarr, by Jonathan Romney, *Enthusiasm*, issue 4, p. 7.

3 I am 32 people

1 Authorship unknown, possibly Austen Williams. Reproduced by kind permission of Mrs Daphne Williams.

2 *Wire in the Blood*, broadcast on ITV, series based on books by Val McDermid.

3 Zadie Smith, *On Beauty* (London, Penguin, 2006), p. 225.

4 Kapka Kassabova, 'Mirages', in *Staying Alive* (Tarset, Bloodaxe Books, 2002). Used by permission of Auckland University Press.

5 Steven Shakespeare and Hugh Rayment-Pickard, 'Inclusive, Confident, Faithful: A Response to Rowan Williams', in *Signs of the Times*, newsletter of the Modern Churchpeople's Union, January 2007, p. 5.

6 Tom Butler, 'Thought for the Day', BBC Radio 4, 21 November 2006.

7 Mitch Albom, *The Five People you Meet in Heaven* (New York, Hyperion Books, 2003), p. 18.

4 More poetry than prose

1 Walter Brueggemann, *The Covenanted Self* (Minneapolis, Fortress Press, 1999), ch. 1.

2 Miroslav Volf, *Exclusion and Embrace: A Theological Exploration of Identity, Otherness and Reconciliation* (Nashville, Abingdon Press, 1996).

5 My parallel lives

1 Jeanette Winterson, *Oranges are Not the Only Fruit* (London/Boston, Pandora Press, 1985).

2 Susan Debnam, *Mine's Bigger than Yours*, from an extract in the *Guardian*, 7 October 2006.

3 Stephanie Dale, *What's Missing from Your Life? – The Men*, broadcast on BBC Radio 4, 5 March 2007.

4 Kirsty Gunn, *Guardian*, 21 February 2007. From Kirsty Gunn, *44 Things: My Year at Home* (London, Atlantic Books, 2007). Copyright © 2007 Kirsty Gunn. Reproduced by permission of the author c/o Rogers, Coleridge & White Ltd, 20 Powis Mews, London W11 1JN.

5 Kirsty Gunn, *Guardian*, 21 February 2007. From Kirsty Gunn, *44 Things: My Year at Home* (London, Atlantic Books, 2007). Copyright © 2007 Kirsty Gunn. Reproduced by permission of the author c/o Rogers, Coleridge & White Ltd, 20 Powis Mews, London W11 1JN.

6 The road not entirely right

1 Matthew 5.48.
2 *The New Jerome Biblical Commentary* (London, Geoffrey Chapman, 1968), p. 644.
3 Louis MacNeice, 'Entirely', in *Staying Alive* (Tarset, Bloodaxe Books, 2002), p. 60. Louis MacNeice, *Collected Poems* (Faber and Faber). Used by permission of David Higham Associates.
4 W. H. Vanstone, *Love's Endeavour, Love's Expense: The Response of Being to the Love of God* (London, Darton, Longman & Todd, 1977), p. 67.
5 Vanstone, *Love's Endeavour*, p. 48.
6 Vanstone, *Love's Endeavour*, p. 63.
7 Vanstone, *Love's Endeavour*, p. 48.
8 Vanstone, *Love's Endeavour*, p. 74.
9 Vanstone, *Love's Endeavour*, p. 74.
10 *The Truth About Size Zero*, broadcast on ITV, 7 March 2007.

7 A green spiral tattoo

1 *The London Challenge 2012* (Diocese of London, 2007).
2 Genesis 1.28; 2.19.
3 Exodus 16.12–18.
4 Leviticus 19.9–10.
5 Leviticus 25.3–5.
6 1 Kings 5; Ezra 1.
7 Gustavo Gutiérrez, *On Job: God-Talk and the Suffering of the Innocent* (Maryknoll, NY, Orbis, 1987).
8 *Sunrise Meditation*, broadcast on BBC Radio 4, Easter Day 2007.
9 Jeffrey Sachs, *Bursting at the Seams*, Reith Lectures: Lecture 1, broadcast on BBC Radio 4, 11 April 2007.
10 Barbara Kingsolver, 'Blueprints', in *Homeland* (London, Faber & Faber, 1989), pp. 26–7.

8 The ordinary magic

1 Martha Beck, *Expecting Adam: A True Story of Birth, Transformation and Unconditional Love* (London, Piatkus, 2000), p. 73.
2 T. S. Eliot, 'The Love Song of J. Alfred Prufrock', in *The Complete Poems and Plays of T. S. Eliot* (London, Faber & Faber, 1969), pp. 13–17. Used by permission.
3 Eliot, 'The Love Song of J. Alfred Prufrock', pp. 13–17. Used by permission.
4 Kathy Galloway, 'Over Coffee', in *Love Burning Deep: Poems and Lyrics* (London, SPCK, 1993), p. 50. Used by kind permission of the author.

5 Matthew 25.1–13.
6 Matthew 24.51.
7 Matthew 25.30.
8 Matthew 25.46.
9 Matthew 25.13.
10 Kathleen Jamie, 'The Way We Live', in *Mr and Mrs Scotland are Dead: Poems 1980–1994* (Tarset, Bloodaxe Books, 2002). Used by permission.
11 *Cities Without Maps*, broadcast on BBC Radio 4, 18 May 2006.
12 Chapter headings from Barbara Glasson's *I am Somewhere Else: Gospel Reflections from an Emerging Church* (London, Darton, Longman & Todd, 2006).
13 Alan Hollinghurst, *The Line of Beauty* (London, Picador, 2004), p. 501.

9 The faint hope of Sabbath

1 Exodus 20.11.
2 Simon Parke, *Church Times*, 13 April 2007.
3 Andrew O'Hagan, *Be Near Me* (London, Faber & Faber, 2006), p. 46.
4 Cambridge Online Dictionary.
5 E. A. Livingstone (ed.), *Concise Oxford Dictionary of the Christian Church* (Oxford, Oxford University Press, 1977), p. 350.

10 Sitting loose to it all

1 Paul Tillich, *The Shaking of the Foundations* (New York, Charles Scribner's Sons, 1955), ch. 11, taken from <http://www.religion-online.org/>.
2 Matthew 11.30.
3 William Temple, *The Hope of a New World* (London, SCM Press, 1940).
4 Alan Brownjohn, 'For a Journey', in *The Nation's Favourite Poems of Journeys* (London, BBC Worldwide, 2000), p. 110. Alan Brownjohn's 'For a Journey' is from his *Collected Poems* (Enitharmon Press, 2006). Used by permission.
5 Matthew 3.13–15.
6 Rebecca Wells, *Little Altars Everywhere* (London, Macmillan, 2000), pp. 313–14.
7 Alice Walker, *The Temple of my Familiar* (London, Women's Press, 1989), p. 146.

11 Losing it entirely

1 The Master of the Life of the Virgin, *The Presentation in the Temple*, National Gallery, London.

2 Luke 2.22–40.
3 Genesis 22.
4 Luke 2.35.
5 John 19.26–27, King James Bible.
6 Raj Persaud, 'One Court Martial Won't Stop all this Brutality', *Independent*, 22 January 2005.
7 Health section of BBC website at <http://www.bbc.co.uk/health/conditions/mental_health/disorders_depression.shtml>.
8 Mark 15.24.
9 Luke 23.28.
10 Bertolt Brecht, *Poems 1913–1956*, 2nd corr. edn, ed. John Willett and Ralph Manheim (London, Methuen, 1979), p. 360. Reproduced by kind permission of A&C Black.

12 'I want to stay here'

1 Emma Chichester Clark, *Up in Heaven* (New York, Random House, 2004).
2 Douglas Board, *The Naked Year: Prayers from the Heart of London* (London, St Martin-in-the-Fields Ltd, 2004), p. 96. Used by permission.
3 Rubem Alves, *Tomorrow's Child: Imagination, Creativity, and the Rebirth of Culture* (New York, Harper & Row, 1972).
4 Sermon preached Easter Day 2006, at St Martin-in-the-Fields.
5 <http://www.museoomero.it/museoomero/>.
6 David Scott, 'Michelangelo's Rondanini Pietà', in *Piecing Together* (Tarset, Bloodaxe Books, 2005), p. 59. Used by permission.
7 John 20.18.
8 Philippians 1.21.
9 Zadie Smith, *On Beauty* (London, Penguin, 2006), p. 69.

13 Six degrees of separation

1 E. M. Forster, *Howards End* (New York, Alfred A. Knopf, 1991), p. 195.
2 Giles Fraser, *Church Times*, 13 April 2007.
3 Helen Simpson, 'Constitutional', in *Constitutional* (London, Jonathan Cape, 2005), pp. 117–18.
4 Matthew 9.20.
5 C. S. Lewis, *The Four Loves* (London, Collins, 1963), pp. 58–9.
6 Rowan Williams, *Silence and Honey Cakes: The Wisdom of the Desert* (Oxford, Lion, 2003), pp. 91–5.

Bibliography

Books

Albom, Mitch, *The Five People you Meet in Heaven*. New York, Hyperion Books, 2003.

Alves, Rubem, *Tomorrow's Child: Imagination, Creativity, and the Rebirth of Culture*. New York, Harper & Row, 1972.

Beck, Martha, *Expecting Adam: A True Story of Birth, Transformation and Unconditional Love*. London, Piatkus, 2000.

Board, Douglas, *The Naked Year: Prayers from the Heart of London*. London, St Martin-in-the-Fields Ltd, 2004.

Bonhoeffer, Dietrich, *Letters and Papers from Prison*, rev. edn, ed. Eberhard Bethge, trans. Reginald Fuller and others. New York, Macmillan, 1967.

Brueggemann, Walter, *The Covenanted Self*. Minneapolis, Fortress Press, 1999.

Chichester Clark, Emma, *Up in Heaven*. New York, Random House, 2004.

Forster, E. M., *Howards End*. New York, Alfred A. Knopf, 1991.

Gallagher, Nora, *Things Seen and Unseen: A Year Lived in Faith*. New York, Vintage Books, 1994.

Glasson, Barbara, *I am Somewhere Else: Gospel Reflections from an Emerging Church*. London, Darton, Longman & Todd, 2006.

Gutiérrez, Gustavo, *On Job: God-Talk and the Suffering of the Innocent*. Maryknoll, NY, Orbis, 1987.

Hollinghurst, Alan, *The Line of Beauty*. London, Picador, 2004.

Irenaeus, *Against Heresies*. Kila, MT, Kessinger, 2004.

Kingsolver, Barbara, 'Blueprints', in *Homeland*. London, Faber & Faber, 1989.

Lewis, C. S., *The Four Loves*. London, Collins, 1963.

O'Hagan, Andrew, *Be Near Me*. London, Faber & Faber, 2006.

Seabright, Paul, *The Company of Strangers*. Princeton, NJ, Princeton University Press, 2005.

Simpson, Helen, *Constitutional*. London, Jonathan Cape, 2005.

Smith, Zadie, *On Beauty*. London, Penguin, 2006.

Temple, William, *The Hope of a New World*. London, SCM Press, 1940.

Thoreau, Henry David, *Walden*. Harmondsworth, Penguin, 1983.

Tillich, Paul, *The Shaking of the Foundations*. New York, Charles Scribner's Sons, 1955.

Tolkien, J. R. R., *The Lord of the Rings, Part Three: The Return of the King.* London, George Allen and Unwin, 1955.

Vanstone, W. H., *Love's Endeavour, Love's Expense: The Response of Being to the Love of God.* London, Darton, Longman & Todd, 1977.

Volf, Miroslav, *Exclusion and Embrace: A Theological Exploration of Identity, Otherness and Reconciliation.* Nashville, Abingdon Press, 1996.

Walker, Alice, *The Temple of my Familiar.* London, Women's Press, 1989.

Wells, Rebecca, *Little Altars Everywhere.* London, Macmillan, 2000.

Williams, Rowan, *Silence and Honey Cakes: The Wisdom of the Desert.* Oxford, Lion, 2003.

Winterson, Jeanette, *Oranges are Not the Only Fruit.* London/Boston, Pandora Press, 1985.

Articles

Debnam, Susan, 'Mine's Bigger than Yours', from an extract in the *Guardian*, 7 October 2006.

Fraser, Giles, *Church Times*, 13 April 2007.

Gunn, Kirsty, 'You Ask Me if I'm Lonely', *Guardian*, 21 February 2007.

Parke, Simon, *Church Times*, 13 April 2007.

Persaud, Raj, 'One Court Martial Won't Stop all this Brutality', *Independent*, 2 January 2005.

Romney, Jonathan, Interview with Béla Tarr, *Enthusiasm*, issue 4.

Shakespeare, Steven and Rayment-Pickard, Hugh, 'Inclusive, Confident, Faithful: A Response to Rowan Williams', in *Signs of the Times*, newsletter of the Modern Churchpeople's Union, January 2007.

Lectures

Sachs, Jeffrey, *Bursting at the Seams*, Reith Lectures, 2007.

Poetry

Astley, Neil (ed.), *Staying Alive*. Tarset, Bloodaxe Books, 2002.

Brecht, Bertolt, *Poems 1913–1956*, 2nd corr. edn, ed. John Willett and Ralph Manheim. London, Methuen, 1979.

Edmond, Lauris, *New and Selected Poems*. Newcastle upon Tyne, Bloodaxe Books, 1992.

Eliot, T. S., 'The Love Song of J. Alfred Prufrock', in *The Complete Poems and Plays of T. S. Eliot*. London, Faber & Faber, 1969.

Galloway, Kathy, *Love Burning Deep: Poems and Lyrics*. London, SPCK, 1993.

Gunn, Kirsty, *44 Things: My Year at Home*. London, Atlantic Books, 2007.

Jamie, Kathleen, *Mr and Mrs Scotland are Dead: Poems 1980–1994*. Tarset, Bloodaxe Books, 2002.

Levertov, Denise, *This Great Unknowing: Last Poems*. Tarset, Bloodaxe Books, 2001.

The Nation's Favourite Poems of Journeys. London, BBC Worldwide, 2000.

Scott, David, *Piecing Together*. Tarset, Bloodaxe Books, 2005.

Williams, Austen, 'I am two people' (original title 'I am two men'), in a probably unpublished sermon from St Martin-in-the-Fields.

Radio and television broadcasts

All Things Considered, broadcast on BBC Radio Wales, 19 March 2006.

Cities Without Maps, broadcast on BBC Radio 4, 18 May 2006.

Sunrise Meditation, broadcast on Radio 4, Easter Day 2007.

'Thought for the Day' with Tom Butler, BBC Radio 4, 21 November 2006.

The Truth About Size Zero, broadcast on ITV, 7 March 2007.

What's Missing from Your Life? – The Men, by Stephanie Dale, BBC Radio 4, 5 March 2007.

Wire in the Blood, broadcast on ITV, series based on books by Val McDermid.

Reference works

Cambridge Online Dictionary.

The New Jerome Biblical Commentary. London, Geoffrey Chapman, 1968.

Livingstone, E. A. (ed.), *Concise Oxford Dictionary of the Christian Church*. Oxford, Oxford University Press, 1977.

Wikipedia.

Websites

www.bbc.co.uk/health/conditions/mental_health/disorders_depression.shtml

www.museoomero.it/museoomero/

Other media

The London Challenge 2012, DVD. London, Diocese of London, 2007.